THE POLITICAL C
OF THE REFO]

MICHAEL SHARPE

Published by the Reform Club, 104 Pall Mall, London SW1Y 5EW

Copyright© Michael Sharpe 1996

Printed by Silhouette Print Ltd, Burnham Trading Estate,
Burnham Road, Dartford, Kent DA1 5BH

ISBN: 0 9503053 2 4

CONTENTS

Foreword	i
Preface	iii
INTRODUCTION	1

1 THE EARLY YEARS
   Founding Of The Club   7
   A Dominant Whiggism   14
   Towards A Political Committee   18

2 FORMATION OF THE POLITICAL COMMITTEE
   Composition And Role   23
   Lost Opportunities   27
   Radical Disillusionment   32

3 THE ACTIVE PHASE
   'Interference' In Constituencies   37
   Expulsions On Political Grounds   43
   An Irritated Club Membership And The Chamberlain Affair   51

4 DIVISION AND A RETREAT FROM POLITICS
   The 'Attack' On The Political Committee   56
   The 'Split' Of 1886   62
   In The Wake Of The First Home Rule Bill   68

5 A REVISED ROLE AND A CHANGING MEMBERSHIP
   Dinners Of A 'Political Character'   73
   A Changing Membership   78
   A Continuing Relevance?   86

CONCLUSION	90
Appendices	95
Abbreviations	107
Bibliography	108

Foreword
by Professor Lord Beloff, F.B.A.

As someone who has had the good fortune of passing many weeks of his working life in recent years between Sir Charles Barry's two masterpieces, the Palace of Westminster and the Reform Club, and as a long time member of the Club's Political Committee, it gives me the greatest pleasure to commend this history of the Committee to a wider readership. It should attract attention well outside the Club's own membership as an important contribution to our knowledge of the inner working of the British party system over a significant part of the nineteenth century and the early part of the present one. The clubs of London's West End have no parallel in any other western capital where such clubs as do exist are purely social and have never been part of the political scene. Yet as is well known the origins of the London clubs were not political but directed to the provision of gambling facilities for nobles and gentlemen. In time some of these clubs where they survived acquired some political flavour - the elegant Whiggism of Brooks's or the ingrained Toryism of White's. The Reform Club itself belongs to a second generation when clubs with a predetermined political slant were established, as well as others catering to different branches of the public service and some of the professions. It is clubs such as these in Pall Mall, St. James's Street and St. James's Square that gave rise to the concept of clubland where political news and gossip first found a hearing and where the men on the make and the wirepullers who would help to determine their success or failure could be found, wining, dining and talking or perusing the newspapers specifically directed at such a clientele. The world of the Tadpoles and Tapers was the world they knew.

What Michael Sharpe shows in his most original study is that where the Reform Club was concerned the Club and its committees and in particular the Political Committee played a central part in the creation of the combination of Whigs and Radicals that formed the nucleus of the progressive wing of British politics eventually transformed into the modern Liberal Party by the advent of the Peelites.

During the middle decades of the century when party affiliation was added to local distinction or mere merit as the avenue to Parliamentary candidatures, the Political Committee was an active participant in the selection of candidates and in the conduct of their campaigns.

Activity of this kind could not survive the successive expansions of the franchise which called for the organisation of the party faithful on a national scale and the establishment at the centre of supervisory machinery. After the advent of something approaching manhood suffrage the monopolisation of the road to office by a gentlemen's club was bound to give way. What is interesting is the fact that despite the tensions in the Liberal Party, leading to the exodus of the Unionists and competition for the formerly Liberal vote by the new Labour Party (which had no ties with the clubs or clubland), the Reform Club and its Political Committee continued to play a part in the Party's fortunes on a more modest scale by bringing the leadership into closer touch with some of the rank and file. It thus witnessed the decline of the Party reflected in the divisions between coalitionists and "wee frees" so that Asquith became the Club's last and most distinguished alumnus in the political arena. Of a rival club for the allegiance of Liberals it has been reported that the state of play could be determined by whether the portrait of Lloyd George was hung on the wall of its principal room or consigned to the vaults. In any event no-one now seeking to secure the favourable notice of Mr Paddy Ashdown would begin with acquiring membership of the Reform Club or its Political Committee. Of the surviving clubs of the second generation, only the Carlton Club has maintained a direct connection with Conservative Party politics.

What is interesting about the Reform Club today is that it still has a Political Committee though a body of a very different kind. It is now one of a number of what are in effect dining clubs within the larger Club, assembling at regular intervals to hear speakers, normally recruited from outside the Club though not invariably so. The membership of the Political Committee reflects the changing character of the Club's membership - the advent of more public servants, more members of the professions particularly the legal profession, more representatives of commerce and finance and latterly of course more women in all these categories.

What may strike one as curious is that the element most lacking in the Political Committee is the political one. The Reform Club still has members of both Houses of Parliament (and candidates) from all three political parties but they do not on the whole figure in the proceedings of the Political Committee. Since many of its meetings, particularly perhaps those addressed by Ambassadors to the Court of St. James contain material of definite relevance to the political issues of the moment, this is at first sight surprising. But it helps to show how far we have come from the great days of government by gentlemen, and its replacement by government by professional politicians whose fortunes are governed by party machines and whose daily timetables are dictated by the party whips. In my view their incarceration in Barry's other masterpiece is a loss to themselves as well as the Political Committee. Indeed when a member of the House of Commons is invited to speak one can be fairly certain that long before discussion terminates, the invitee will be off to cast his or her (usually otiose) vote in the division lobbies.

Many readers of Michael Sharpe's book may find themselves giving way to feelings of nostalgia and could wish to be transported back to the days when the Political Committee was indeed political, and when the British parliamentary constitution and its habits were the envy of the world.

House of Lords   Beloff
April 1996

PREFACE

The prestige of London's Reform Club, founded in 1836 to service the anti-Conservative alliance (or 'Reform Party') in Parliament, owes much to its reputation among international freedom movements of the 19th Century as a symbol of political progress. The continuing existence of the Club's Political Committee is based on that tradition of interest in foreign as well as home affairs. For the Committee prospers to-day as an exclusive association of up to fifty members of the Reform Club, of whom ten must be elected each year. These meet periodically to dine and discuss current affairs, although the Club, including its Political Committee, now owns to no party political bias describing itself as a 'Social Club for Reformers'.

The research for this account of the role and activities of the Political Committee has proceeded in parallel with the preparation of a dissertation for a Master of Arts degree on the same subject, under the supervision of the History Department at the University of York. A limit of 30,000 words has meant confining the dissertation largely to the period between the establishment of a Political Committee in 1869, and the 'Split' within the membership of both Club and Committee following defeat of Gladstone's 'First Home Rule Bill' In 1886. This more comprehensive account dwells more fully on the origins of the Club itself, and has been extended into the 20th Century. However the dissertation forms its core as, in the years after 1886, with Reformers (or Liberals as they had become known) divided between both Government and Opposition, the Club largely ceased to play an active part in politics.

It has been a privilege to be allowed unrestricted access to the Reform Club's archive, housed in its premises at Pall Mall. I am grateful to Peter Urbach, the current chairman of the Committee responsible for the Club's renowned library, to Simon Blundell, the Club's librarian, who has dealt most patiently and helpfully with all my requests, and to members of the Political Committee itself, for granting me that privilege. I am also grateful for the help provided by Vermica Herrington and Simon Roberts, respectively assistant archivist and secretary of the National Liberal Club, and by Nick Lee and Michael Richardson of the Special Collections Department of the University of Bristol, in which most of that Club's 'Gladstone Library' is now held. Much of the material to which they were kind enough to provide access refers to the period after 1886, but it was of particular help in determining the relationship between Reform and National Liberal Clubs, in providing background for the later sections of this account, and in forming my conclusions.

I should like to thank several other individuals, who have reacted with such courtesy to my approaches for information and for copies of documents. These include Hester Borron, archivist for the Lambton Estate, Melissa

Dalziel of the Bodleian Library, Angus Farquharson of Finzean, Ann Farr of the Brotherton Library at the University of Leeds, Robert Linsley, Secretary of the Carlton Club, Iona Molesworth-St. Aubyn and Maureen Shovell of Pencarrow, Joy Moorhead, Secretary to the Dowager Marchioness of Normanby, Janie Morris, an archivist at North Carolina's Duke University, and Catherine O'Rourke of Wexford County Library. Archivists and librarians of British public authorities, all of whom have responded willingly to requests, include those of the British Library's Department of Western Manuscripts at Great Russell Street, its Newspaper Library at Colindale, the Public Record Office at Kew, the Royal Commission on Historical Manuscripts at Chancery Lane, the Record Office of the House of Lords, Scotland's National Register of Archives and National Library's Department of Manuscripts, both at Edinburgh, and the city/county libraries of Aberdeen, Bristol, Leeds, Manchester and Kent.

Finally, I should like to record my gratitude for all the help I have received during the preparation of the dissertation for my Master of Arts degree from the department of history at my own university, that of York. In particular my tutor, Allen Warren, has spent many hours providing invaluable advice and guiding my research. It is his extensive knowledge of the politics of the period which fired my own enthusiasm.

Malton, North Yorkshire
September 1996

Michael Sharpe

INTRODUCTION

The founding of clubs with political aims was hardly a new idea at the time of the 'First (or Great) Reform Act' of 1832. Earlier 17th and 18th Century examples were Major Wildman's 'Republican Club' (1658), the Whig 'Green Ribbon Club' (1674), the Country Party's 'October Club' (1710) and the Tory 'Cocoa Tree Club' (1727). Members met to pass the time dining, wining, gaming, talking scandal, lampooning political leaders and plotting against, or on behalf of, the House of Stuart. Surroundings were plain, the food and its presentation that of the coffee house or tavern, and the atmosphere over-warm and no doubt conducive to the liberal application of scent. By the dawn of the 19th Century such institutions were better housed, if still not adequately ventilated. Most had largely developed into exclusive gaming clubs such as Boodles (1762), or those which retained a political bias such as Brooks's (1764), the social centre for Whigs.

Growth of empire, industry and the world of finance, accelerated by the commanding place of Britain in the councils of Europe following the Napoleonic wars, led to the founding of a new group of clubs. Most of these were designed to service the enlarged professions or imperial interests, for example the United Service (1815), Travellers (1819), Athenaeum (1824), Oriental (1824) and City of London (1832). It followed that aspiring politicians from the expanding professions, unable to join the relatively small and exclusive politically inclined clubs of the day, were receptive to the idea of political clubs of their own in both London and the provinces. Perhaps of more significance, the more astute among their political leaders soon realised that organisation was needed to cope with the introduction of compulsory registration for an enlarged electorate contained within the legislation of the Reform Act of 1832. An headquarters was needed to provide the link between leaders and the led, to maximise the vote, and to co-ordinate this process between constituencies. The Tories, sharpened by Opposition after some twenty years in power, were quickest off the mark with the Carlton. That Club opened its doors in 1832, drawing its membership immediately from a wide (in early 19th Century terms) social spectrum of supporters.

Few historians have made more than a passing reference to political clubs. One who did so is Professor Norman Gash. He devoted a chapter to the subject, which he headed 'Club Government', in his <u>Politics In The Age Of Peel: a Study in the Technique of Parliamentary Democracy</u>, but largely limited his discussion to the period between the 'First Reform Act' and 1850. An opportunity has now arisen to take the subject of the role of a metropolitan political club into the second half of the 19th Century, and beyond. The early decades of this period are of particular interest in the context of the Reform Club. For they included the formation of its Political Committee against a background in which politics became a major

1

preoccupation of the nation, the professional and commercial middle classes increasingly took their place within the House of Commons, the Ballot was introduced, and two further Reform Acts enlarged the electorate to almost six million, that is to say from one in five to two out of every three adult males. It was also the period in which the issue of the political integrity of the United Kingdom split the governing (Liberal) Party, thereby handing the high ground of politics to its Conservative opponent for all but three of the following twenty years.

The part played by the Carlton and Reform Clubs in the development of the Conservative and Liberal (as it became known) Parties is not particularly well documented. The files of the Carlton Club were lost in October 1940 as a result of enemy action, and while there is some surviving correspondence of a political nature from members within the archive of the Reform Club, this is largely confined to the last decade of the 19th and to the 20th Centuries. Thus in examining the work of the latter's Political Committee it has been necessary to rely primarily on minute books which are written in the customary shorthand style of such records. Nevertheless, much of substance can be gleaned using the Club's own letter and candidate books, the biographical records of members, and by cross referencing with the minutes of other committees and of general meetings. National and local press accounts of contemporary events, and the published reminiscences and private letters of members held within both private and public archives, have been useful. Journals such as Nineteenth Century and the Quarterly Review have provided further information in the shape of contemporary articles written by members. From such primary sources It has been possible to establish a pattern to the political role of the Reform Club, and to hazard some conclusions as to its significance within a changing Liberal Party.

Use of the word 'Liberal' to describe the 'ill assorted alliance' of parliamentary Radicals, Whigs, Irish repealers, and those who already referred to themselves as Liberals, under Whig leadership, was already widespread by the mid 1830s. Liberalism had evolved as an attitude of mind rather than doctrine, a belief in a practical freedom under the law and in the discovery of solutions for society through the power of reason and debate by an enlightened political group. Even the majority of parliamentary Radicals of the 1830s were Utilitarians 'seeking the greatest happiness of the greatest number'. While promoting further Reform through a more broadly based electorate, they remained suspicious of the potential for tyranny which might flow from too much enfranchisement of a largely uneducated majority. The revolutionary example of France was a powerful reminder of the effects of such democracy, and it is certainly true that parliamentary Radicals of this period, while detesting the arrogant elitism of Whiggery and determined to secure a more equitable share of political power, supported private rights and security of property over the redistribution of wealth.

It may be useful in following the political role of the Reform Club, and its association with the fortunes of the Liberal Party, to be able to refer occasionally to a list of governing Administrations following the Reform Act of 1832. Such a list, which includes short explanatory notes on the introduction to the political scene of the descriptions 'Conservative' and 'Liberal', is therefore included at Appendix 1. However, it should be noted that the choice of 'label' applied to each Administration, particularly those around the middle of the 19th Century, is based on a subjective judgement of the overall thrust of its leadership. Party discipline was very loose during the 1850s and much of the 1860s, following the 'Split' in the Conservative Party over Repeal of the Corn Laws, and the period saw the introduction of such terms as 'Liberal-Conservative' and 'Conservative-Liberal'. Indeed Gladstone, himself, referred contemporaneously to a "greatly narrowed interval" between the two main political groupings in an article which he wrote in 1856 for the Quarterly Review, under a heading of 'The Declining Efficiency of Parliament'. Nevertheless, by 1867, the 'phoney war' was over, in no small part due to the style of leadership provided for their respective parties by Disraeli and Gladstone.

Born of a parliamentary Radical initiative in 1836, the Reform Club soon settled down as the primary metropolitan institution from which the parliamentary whips and party organisers of the anti-Tory or anti-Conservative 'alliance' recruited and managed MPs, serviced the growing number of constituency associations, and co-ordinated the fighting of elections. In short it acted as a party political headquarters in the organisational sense, although that term applied very loosely during much of the 19th Century with constituencies quick to protect their local independence. Membership of the Reform was drawn from a wider social and even religious background than was normal for the Clubs of London at the time. The Club's growing status abroad in an increasingly egalitarian Europe and aggressively democratic United States, its reputation for civilised fellowship at home and not least its magnificent cuisine, added to its attraction. Once the divisive issue of repeal of the Corn Laws had been consigned to history in 1846, calls for active support in the cause of progressive reforming politics seem to have met with little enthusiasm from a membership understandably inclined to avoid disharmony.

Such an attitude at the heart of the parliamentary party can only have been reinforced by the politically shrewd, relaxed and popular leadership of Lord Palmerston. Middle class Radicalism was provided with a share of the spoils of office and, in the process, merged with a 'lukewarm' mainstream Liberalism which was largely content to pursue a limited political programme. Only a relatively small number of parliamentary Liberals seem to have been alive to the increasing interdependence between local association and member of parliament, particularly in the fast growing borough constituencies, and to the challenge provided by new more progressive and articulate Radical lobbies not least those concerned with promoting the interests of organised labour. The formation of a Political Committee in the wake of the opportunistic Disraeli's Reform Act of 1867, some thirty-three years after the founding of the Club, and following previous abortive efforts to galvanise members into action, was probably the high point of this minority's efforts. It came too late to make a marked impact. The days of so-called Club Government were over in the new era of Gladstonian Liberalism which followed the death of Palmerston in 1865, and Liberal victory in the general election of 1868.

The Political Committee's terms of reference were primarily concerned with the organisation of party and of parliamentary candidates for elections. Efforts to this end were not helped by much of the legislation of Gladstone's first Administration (1868-1874), which succeeded effectively in the progressive alienation of much of its Nonconformist, temperance and trade unionist support. Following Conservative success and the return of Disraeli as Prime Minister at the general election of 1874, action was taken to improve co-ordination at the centre by combining the parliamentary whips' office and Registration Association into a Liberal Central Association. Cross fertilisation between members of the new organisation's Executive Committee and those of the Political Committee of the Reform Club was put in hand at the initiative of the latter.

Nevertheless, such 'tinkering' at the centre was hardly more than an attempt to fight the organisational battles of the past. By the mid 1870s there were two possible courses of action facing such a diverse and fragmented institution as the Liberal Party. Unify under the banner of some great moral issue, the option followed with such success by Gladstone in the late 1870s, with his successful campaign against Disraeli's imperial rhetoric and its concomitant 'corruption' of society, and/or reorganise party and policy from the grassroots, the course taken by Joseph Chamberlain leading to the foundation in 1877 of the National Liberal Federation. Yet neither were enough to offset the frustrations and divisions of Gladstone's second Administration (1880-1885), nor to keep the Party together over his apparently sudden commitment to Home Rule for Ireland in 1886. The majority of the Political Committee did, however, remain loyal to Gladstone. In doing so the Committee reflected the views of most members of the Reform Club as well as those of the parliamentary party, but a significant minority in both felt unable to accept Home Rule.

There is clear evidence of a continuing perception within constituencies, borne out by articles in Radical and provincial journals, of the Reform Club as an exclusive institution. Such an attitude played its part in attributing to the Club a sense of mystery, and therefore a rather more important role in the affairs of the Liberal Party than is justified. This is certainly true of the era following the establishment of the Political Committee, an era in which the making of policy was retained firmly in the hands of Gladstone and a handful of close colleagues in the Cabinet. Whig numerical superiority within Liberal

Cabinets until 1886, and the close association between a Liberal Central Association, controlled by the whips, and the Political Committee played their part. Social considerations, such as long waiting lists reflecting the desirability of a membership which included many of the party's grandees, were no doubt another factor.

The Political Committee provided speakers for public meetings, raised funds at general elections, found parliamentary candidates with the necessary wealth when asked to do so and, more controversially, sought to arbitrate between Liberals competing for the same parliamentary seat. Somewhat ill advisedly it also seems to have acted as the initiator of resolutions to expel members of the Club for political disloyalty. Yet there are signs throughout that the membership of the Club as a whole was reluctant to support any but the most bland initiative of a political nature. By 1884 this reluctance had contributed to a growing deterioration in relations between General and Political Committees. This culminated in a resolution at the Annual General Meeting of May 1885, albeit an unsuccessful one, to abolish the latter.

It took over thirty years for the members of the Reform Club to establish a Political Committee, but only a further seventeen to come to the conclusion that the plurality of politics within the Liberal Party and the ethos of Club were too strong a mixture. In 1886 the Club ceased to play an active part in party politics, although it continued to retain much of its significance as a symbol of traditional Liberalism. In the years after 1886 the Political Committee, reflecting within its ranks a divided Liberal Party, managed to survive but only by taking little action other than to perpetuate its own existence. Interestingly this was a path which the National Liberal Club, founded less than a decade before, declined to follow, yet its Political Committee also survived. The circumstances under which both did so will be examined, as will eventual rediscovery on the part of the Political Committee of the Reform Club of a role for itself in 1911. This followed acceptance of the chairmanship by the then Liberal leader and Prime Minister, Herbert Asquith. Even this redefined role, as organising committee for a series of dinners of a 'political character', was not agreed without apprehension, even hostility, on the part of some members of the Club. At least initially, these included some of those serving on its General Committee.

It will be seen that members were more than ever concerned not to prejudice personal relationships within the Club's walls, or the size of the candidates' list, through over-enthusiastic political partisanship. This was a situation which reflected new divisions among Liberals. However, there is little doubt of the success of the Political Committee's promotion of a series of glittering social occasions. Some of these had political significance as a platform for individual Liberal leaders. Others were part of an attempt to keep the flag of Reform flying in the company of industrialists, scientists, and the world of the arts, a role that continues to this day although specifically without party political affiliation. For it was during the period between the general election of October 1924, which saw a fall in Liberal representation In the House of Commons to only forty seats, and the general election of October 1931 fought by Liberals as three separate factions, that the Club openly accepted that to be a Reformer it was not necessary to be a political Liberal.

Concentration primarily upon the Club's Political Committee means devoting most time to the period between 1869 and 1886, when its members were at their most politically active. However, in order to clarify the committee's role, it is necessary to start by placing the Reform Club itself within the context of a developing Liberal Party. The reasons behind, and consequences of, the political 'modus vivendi' of 1886, reached within the Club in response to the introduction by Gladstone of his divisive policy of Home Rule for Ireland, will be discussed. Finally, the long process of disengagement from active party politics on the part of the Club, and indeed of its Political Committee, as further division among Liberals contributed to a parliamentary party merely a shadow of its former self, will also be examined.

1 THE EARLY YEARS.

Founding of the Club

Some four years after the 'Great Reform Act' of 1832 altered the balance within the Constitution in favour of an elected House of Commons, a small group of parliamentary Radicals took the initiative in the founding of the Reform Club. The need for a parliamentary headquarters had been given a new urgency by the formation of the anti-Conservative alliance of Radicals, Whigs, and Daniel O'Connell's Irish repealers, created by the 'Lichfield House Compact' of February 1835. The Whig leadership, largely convinced that the process of Reform had gone quite far enough, remained content with their citadel of Brooks's. By and large most Whigs were disinclined to 'grub about' in the mechanical arts of party organisation or administration, and could foresee that the establishment of a new Club with a broadly based membership was likely to increase the influence of their more militant or Radical 'partners'. In any case a basic tenet of Whig philosophy was that of the power of individual reason and debate, a concept which might reasonably be claimed at that time to be incompatible with an institution primarily ,aimed at the creation of a form of collective machinery for drumming up party political support. Unsurprisingly this suspicion of organisation was not shared by parliamentary Radicals, buoyed up by electoral success and convinced that the more efficient the electoral net the greater their support. Most Radicals, limited by a relative absence of wealth and status, were compelled to use private residences in which to meet. The founding of the Westminster Club in 1834, renamed the Westminster Reform Club a year later and housed for a rent of six hundred and fifty guineas in part of a Radical MP's residence at 24 Great George Street, illustrates the less than satisfactory arrangements open to Radicals. The Club, which never exceeded a membership of two hundred, closed in 1838 some two years after the founding of the Reform had effectively 'poached' those who remained of its dwindling numbers.[1]

The key to a successful political club lay in persuading the wealthy and largely aristocratic leadership to join. These would attract the ambitious and able thereby encouraging a large membership by providing it with the opportunity to rub shoulders with the great and talented at an affordable cost. Thus a party of Reformers, or Liberals as many were increasingly to name themselves from the 1830s, needed the Whig element if they were to found a successful socio-political institution. Equally, following defeat at the general election of December 1834 at the hands of Sir Robert Peel, many Whigs recognised that they must have the political support of Radicals if they were to maintain themselves as the governing elite. Open voting and registration of electors in the counties meant that such constituencies were vulnerable to the influence of Tory parson and squire, while bribery could neutralise potential

1 Reform Club, Westminster Reform Club Committee Minute Books, 10 December 1837 and 9 May 1838.

anti-Conservative majorities in many borough seats. With the 'Lichfield House Compact', the Whigs had succeeded in welding a winning anti-Conservative alliance into place, but the need for some form of parliamentary party headquarters to service such an ill-assorted grouping had become even more evident at least in Radical minds. Brooks's really was totally unsuitable for the purpose. The Whigs would not tolerate the numbers involved, leaving aside the inevitable change such an influx would have on the socially exclusive nature of the Club. Many Radicals, particularly among Nonconformists, were prevented by their beliefs from entering a gaming club. In any case, Brooks's was too expensive.[2]

The actual process of the founding of the Reform Club was one rooted in antipathy between Whigs and parliamentary Radicals, notwithstanding their political alliance. In spite of ostensibly well-founded later 19th Century accounts, which 'awarded' the title of founder to Edward Ellice MP,[3] there is now no doubt that the driving force behind the Club's foundation was the first Earl of Durham.[4] He was supported by such prominent parliamentary Radicals as the 'Whig hating' baronet, Sir William Molesworth, the Benthamite or Utilitarian Radical leader, Joseph Hume, the philosopher and historian, George Grote and, although not an MP, the lawyer and administrative Reformer, Joseph Parkes, a close associate of the Earl of Durham. Analysis by Professor Gash of the correspondence of Durham, Molesworth, Parkes, and of Edward Ellice himself, shows clearly the scope of manoeuvring on the part of a relatively small group of Radicals designed finally to 'trap' the Whigs into a joint venture.[5]

In particular Durham had been urging the need for a club to embrace all anti-Tories for some years. In the absence of much enthusiasm for the project in Whig circles, but with the help of Parkes, he had therefore set up a Reform Association to co-ordinate the registration of voters through political associations in constituencies, before leaving for St Petersburg as Ambassador-extraordinary in July 1835. In Russia he was kept regularly

---

2 Sir William Molesworth to Mary, Lady Molesworth, 19 February 1835, MoP mss., unreferenced. See also Mrs Fawcett, Life Of The Right Hon. Sir William Molesworth, Bart., MP, FRS (London, 1901), p.74.

3 Louis Fagan, The Reform Club: its Founders and Architect (London, 1887), p.33. W Fraser Rae, 'The Jubilee Of The Reform Club', Nineteenth Century, XIX (1886) p.674. Edward Ellice (1781-1863) was married to the younger sister of the second Earl Grey and opposed to further Reform following his role as Grey's Chief Whip at the time of the Act of 1832. Associated with both Whigs and Radicals he was certainly well placed to act as a bridge between them, and this appears to have been his true role.

4 John George Lambton, 1st Earl of Durham (1792-1840) was socially well-connected and acquired considerable wealth from coal mines on his estates in the North of England. Married to a daughter of Earl Grey in 1816, a member of Grey's Cabinet from 1830 to 1833 and one of its more advanced proponents of Reform. Created Earl of Durham 1833.

5 N Gash, Politics In The Age of Peel: a Study in the Technique of Parliamentary Representation 1830-1850 (London, 1961), Chapter 15.

informed by Parkes of the Association's progress, and also with continuing efforts to form a Club.⁶ By February 1836 the patience of a number of Radicals over the latter issue had reached breaking point. Five MPs, including Molesworth, Hume, and Grote, and two others of whom one was Parkes, issued a public circular on 2 February some forty-eight hours before the opening of the parliamentary session. The circular baldly announced the founding of a Club for Reformers with a list attached of some fifty names as members of its first committee. Molesworth wrote subsequently that none of the fifty had been consulted, but claimed that the majority were MPs known to be sympathetic to the idea of a club.⁷ In a letter to Durham, dated 1 March 1836, Parkes included the names of Molesworth and Grote as prime movers in this enterprise and also enclosed a 'press minute' signed jointly by Molesworth and himself, which Durham acknowledged and returned with his reply. The minute, dated 7 February 1836, records the details of a meeting between the two of them and Ellice and Edward Stanley, the latter then Patronage Secretary (or Chief Whip) to Lord Melbourne's Administration. This meeting was held at Parkes's house in Great George Street on 5 February, three days after issue of the circular announcing the founding of the Club. An angry Ellice is recorded as reproaching Molesworth for being secretive over plans to form a club, while maintaining that there was considerable opposition to the project among Reformers in the House of Commons. Parkes and Molesworth are reported as having riposted that Ellice had been repeatedly approached on the subject, had always been obstructive, that most prominent Radicals did approve of the project, and that they were determined to press ahead: "... the Liberals could and would form it, whether the Whigs would or would not join, but both as distinctly stated their desire and the expediency of a junction with the Whigs, and that a club should be formed comprehending all classes of Liberals ... Ellice then sat at the table, and commenced writing a list of names for the provisional committee ... mutual concessions were made, and the list was finally written out by Mr Ellice".⁸ Ellice's reluctance to become involved until convinced, some might say bluffed, that the Club would go ahead with or without Whig backing, is borne out by one of his own letters to Parkes apparently written at the very beginning of 1836:

> "...I have written to Jo Hume about his club...we should rather endeavour by degrees to enlarge the foundations of our Reform

---

6 Stuart J Reid, *Life and Letters of The First Earl of Durham 1792-1840* (2 vols., London, 1906), Vol.II, pp.3 and 74.

7 Molesworth to Mary, Lady Molesworth, February 1836, MoP mss., unreferenced and with precise date unreadable. See also Mrs Fawcett, *Life Of Molesworth*, p. 76.

8 Joseph Parkes to Durham, 1 March 1836, enclosing minute of 7 February signed by Molesworth and Parkes, Durham to Parkes, 20 March 1836, DP, LEA mss., unreferenced. See also Reid, *Life and Letters of The First Earl Of Durham* Vol.II, pp. 77-80.

association, than risk the failure of a greater speculation under present circumstances. I have serious doubts as to whether any attempt to carry this club system further would be popular - and how far, many of the Town Councils would be frightened by the cry that would be immediately set up of "club government"..."[9]

Whether Ellice genuinely feared such an attitude within constituencies as early as 1836, or was reflecting overall Whig suspicion of any institution likely to encourage Radical influence, is a matter of speculation. It is clear that, once he was persuaded there was no alternative, he and Stanley moved quickly in an attempt to regain control and 'make the best of a bad job'. For one day after their 'confrontation' with Molesworth and Parkes a meeting was called at Fendall's Hotel in New Palace Yard at which it was resolved unanimously:

> "1st. That a Club consisting of Reformers only be forthwith established in the Metropolis to be called The Reform Club for the purpose of bringing together the Reformers of the United Kingdom ..."

A second resolution appointed a provisional committee of thirty-five to organise and establish the Club. The names of these were listed and included thirty-three MPs, of whom some twenty were Radicals. On the same day, 6 February 1836, each member of the provisional committee was summoned by the hastily appointed honorary secretary in a letter headed 'The Reform Club':

> "This Committee being appointed to meet on Monday next, the 8th instant I have to request your attendance at Mr Ellice's house, No. 14 Carlton House Terrace at 2 o'clock - You are particularly requested to meet the other Members of the Committee in order that no time may be lost in carrying into effect the object of these Resolutions..." [10]

Ellice went on to secure the agreement of Whig leaders to the project, and acceptance of membership by the majority of Lord Melbourne's Administration. The first formal meeting of the Club's General Committee was held on 5 May and the Club opened on the 24th of that month, the 17th birthday of the Princess Victoria.

Thus while the driving force behind the belated founding of the Reform Club seems to have been Durham, supported in particular by Molesworth, Parkes and Hume, the 'bridge' between these and the Whig membership which secured the immediate success of the Club was largely provided by

---

9 Edward Ellice to Parkes, EP, NLS mss. 15044, undated but marked 1836 in different handwriting, ff.23/24.

10 John Ashton Yates to Edward Stanley, 6 February 1836, enclosing copy of resolutions passed at the meeting on Saturday 6 February 1836. This original of the letter sent to each member of the Committee is part of the Sir Edward John Stanley Papers held by the Special Collections Library of Duke University, North Carolina.

Edward Ellice and Edward Stanley. Others made a significant contribution, for example Henry Ward, the wealthy businessman and Radical MP for Sheffield, also likely to have been closely associated with the events of early February 1836. He wrote to the Earl of Mulgrave as early as January 1835 asking for his support for a Liberal Club to serve as a "counterpoise" to the Carlton Club. In his letter Ward added that in his opinion:

"...this is impossible to do unless a certain number of the Old Whigs will give their sanction ... by placing their names at the head of the List...if Lord Durham, alone, for instance, were to do so...the Club would represent his opinions and his opinions only. That we do not want. We wish to give it the most extended basis possible among Reformers...we can do no good by forming a Club of this description unless a number of the influential members of Brooks's, at once, take part in it...depend upon it, it would prove a most formidable engine in the event of another Dissolution."[11]

Ward's letter provides a good illustration of the danger of placing parliamentary Whigs and Radicals in separate compartments. As might be expected the dividing line was frequently blurred. Many individuals had a foot in both camps, not least Durham and Ellice. A number of Whigs were to obtain impeccable Radical credentials during the 1840s through support for the abolition of the Corn Laws, for example Charles Villiers, for twenty-six years Chairman of the Reform Club's Political Committee.[12] Joseph Parkes was a Radical and leading administrator in the world of political reform, but he was closely associated with the Whig whips and believed in the constitutional tradition of an enlightened political elite. From the tone and content of Henry Ward's letter it is reasonable to assume that he did not class Mulgrave as a 'died in the wool' Whig, while he is clearly concerned not to allow Durham's mercurial temperament and volatile Radicalism to dominate. Admittedly the first fifty years at least of the Reform Club's existence do reflect division between Whigs and Radicals within a developing Liberal Party. Perhaps of more significance the record tends to show that the majority of members were content with the title of Reformer or that of Liberal; although events combined with the ethos of club life were largely to blur the political zeal implicit in the former description! There seems to be no record of Mulgrave's reply to Ward but, together with the Earl of Durham, Duke of Norfolk, Edward Ellice and General Sir R Ferguson MP, he became an original Trustee of the Club thus confirming his active support for the project. During the next two decades, until the formation of the Liberal Registration Association in 1860, the Club became the centre for such

11 *Henry Ward to Earl of Mulgrave, 22 January 1835, MuP, mss. 0/887.*

12 *Charles Pelham Villiers (1802-1898). Grandson of the First Earl of Clarendon. Leading exponent of free trade and of repeal of the Corn Laws. Classed as a Liberal Unionist after 1886. Elected to the Reform Club in 1836, an original member of its Political Committee and Chairman of that Committee from 1872 for twenty-six years until his death at the age of ninety-six.*

parliamentary Whig-Radical-Reformer-Liberal party political organisation as did exist.

It is likely that Radicals also played a major part in the Club's early life. Some one-third of the thirty members of the first formally elected General Committee were firm parliamentary Radicals, including H A Aglionby, John Crawfurd, George Grote, Joseph Hume, William Molesworth, Henry Warburton, Henry Ward and two Irishmen, Daniel O'Connell himself and Barry O'Meara. At least a further five were staunch adherents of an extension of the suffrage, the Ballot and of shorter parliaments.[13] The choice of title for the Club, attributed to a suggestion by Joseph Hume, was redolent of unfinished business rather than one which suggested that the process of Reform might have gone far enough, while each candidate for membership had to be vouched for as a Reformer by both his proposer and seconder. Admittedly, the word 'Reformer' seems never to have been defined in formal terms, although it is reasonable to assume that those using it would have described themselves as willing to press for such constitutional changes as they considered might be of benefit to the national interest. Certainly, it was the only arbiter of eligibility under the rules which declared the Club's purpose to be that of promoting the social intercourse of the Reformers of the United Kingdom.[14] Commercial or professional success in a broad range of occupations seems to have been as equal a criterion for membership as birth, rather unusually among major London clubs of the time. "A barrister, a physician, or a clergyman might be elected [to the clubs of London]...; but a merchant, an attorney, a surgeon, an architect might knock in vain".[15]

Nevertheless, the number of parliamentary Radical members within the Club's General Committee waned over the next few years, a reflection of their declining numbers in the House of Commons. Contrasting the early hopes of Radicals with their status by the early 1840s, Professor Gash comments that "the numbers and material prosperity guaranteed to the club by the Whig membership could not fail to be without its silent insidious effect on the political independence of the Radicals...The single-mindedness, the integrity, the characteristic acidity of the Radicals that flourished in splendid isolation, could not easily survive transplantation to the convivial atmosphere of the Pall Mall clubrooms".[16] Certainly Radical ideas appear to have been in danger

---

[13] These figures show a disproportionate Radical influence. In comparative terms they exceed even the most optimistic estimate of Radical strength among the 'allies' in the House of Commons in 1836 as being that of 80 Radicals to 152 Whigs and 100 Liberals. See T H Duncombe, (ed.), *The Life and Correspondence of Thomas Slingsby Duncombe Late MP for Finsbury* (2 vols., London, 1868), Vol. 1, p.212, N Gash, *Reaction and Reconstruction in English Politics 1832-1852 The Ford Lectures Delivered In The University of Oxford in The Hilary Term 1964* (Oxford, 1965), p.168.

[14] Reid, *Life and Letters of the First Earl of Durham*, Vol. II, p.74, W Fraser Rae, 'Jubilee of the Reform Club', *Nineteenth Century*, XIX (1886) pp.674-675. According to Rae other titltes discussed included Fox, Hampden, Grey and Milton.

[15] W Besant, *Fifty Years Ago* (London, 1888), p.177.

[16] Gash, *Politics In The Age Of Peel*. p.410, See also D Southgate, *The Passing Of The Whigs 1832-1866* (London, 1962), p. 70. Southgate maintains that "instead of a base headquarters of radicalism the Club became a serviceable extension of the whips' office".

from Whig manners and social influence, as several contemporary writers also bore witness.[17] Following the election of club committees in May 1842, most Radical members of these had been replaced by 'mainstream' Liberals or those 'of Whig principles'.

There was also an essential paradox within the concept of a major London club formed for political ends, which is perhaps absent from one which exists to bring together individuals of similar professional backgrounds from outside the world of politics. Members of the latter tended to treat the subject of politics with a certain degree of wariness, instinctively recognising the strong divisions of opinion likely to surface from time to time and the potential damage these might cause to the collective ethos of club life. Such divisions were always likely in the Reform which embraced within its membership such a diverse political alliance, particularly at a time when politics was becoming a major topic of public interest. In his history of the Travellers Club, written in 1927, Sir Almeric Fitzroy wrote of social gratification as the ruling impulse within the institution of a club. "By a process of natural selection the atmosphere of a Club tends to eliminate qualities hostile to what is described as a clubbable disposition and to foster those favourable to its growth, among which courtesy, accessibility and tact are most prominent".[18] Such an atmosphere would certainly have tended to blunt the truculent, even bigoted, tendency of many Radical reformers of the mid and later 19th Century. Often these pursued cherished, but narrowly based, individual social or political reforms to the detriment of wider reformist, or Liberal party, ideals.

It follows that the pursuit of politics across such a wide range of views, as the primary raison d'etre for its existence, was likely to throw considerable strains on the personal relationships of members of a great Club such as the Reform. Louis Fagan, writing in commemoration of its Golden Jubilee, was to boast that the Club had not reproduced the dissensions of the Liberal Party. "...it [the Club] has continued to shelter 'Adullamites' and 'Radicals', 'Liberal Unionists' and 'Gladstonians'...a place where all shades and grades of Liberalism are brought together in friendly intercourse..."[19] Within the context and timing of his authorship, a loyal club member of such long standing and firm Victorian Liberal beliefs can be excused for indulging himself with a touch of 'the wish being father to the thought'. While the Club did indeed continue to 'shelter' all shades of Liberal opinion, it is hard to accept that this was necessarily in 'friendly intercourse'. Members were often sharply divided on issues and even on the merits of an active political role. In 1886 they largely fell silent on the whole subject of politics for some twenty-five years, in

---

17 The most often recorded comment is that of Henry Rawson, Proprietor of the Morning Star and Secretary of the Anti Corn Law League, to John Bright: "John, John, how can we keep honest if we live in such palaces as this ?", but there are other just as pointed references. See Sir A West, Recollections 1832 to 1886. second ed. (2 vols., London, 1899), Vol.I, p.303, T H Duncombe (ed.), Life and Correspondence of Thomas Slingsby Duncombe, Vol.I, p.67, A Adburgham, A Radical Aristocrat: the Right Hon Sir William Molesworth Bart. PC. MP of Pencarrow and his Wife Andalusia (Padstow, 1990), p.34.

18 Sir Almeric Fitzroy, History of the Travellers Club (London, 1927), p.150.

19 Fagan, The Reform Club. p.137.

order to ensure the continued survival of the Club. 'Shelter' had indeed been bought but at the cost of fundamental change to the Club's raison-d'etre, initially as the forerunner of a party political headquarters, as a Liberal political club, and to the Radical Reformist nature of its political conception.

A Dominant Whiggism

While there is little doubt of the socially exclusive nature of Whig leadership or cousinhood, there are differences of emphasis among historians over the political character of Whiggism. Professor Newbould has suggested that political Whiggism provided a genuine middle ground between Radicals and Tories.[20] Such an argument is consistent with the later 'absorption' within the Liberal Party of a number of parliamentary followers of Sir Robert Peel, including Gladstone, following the split in the Conservative Party over repeal of the Corn Laws, and emphasises the idea of Whig political conservatism. Richard Brent has drawn attention to the continuity of an earlier dimension of Whiggism, that of support for civil and religious liberties and resistance to arbitrary power under the constitution of the 'Glorious Revolution' of 1688. This is a Whiggism which he describes as 'Constitutional Moralism' or 'Liberal Anglicanism'.[21] Yet Dr Jenkins has recently warned against exaggerating the continuity of Whiggism, pointing to a number of examples of 'political fluidity', even of support for the power of the Crown among leading Whig families.[22] Professor Vincent, writing nearly thirty years ago, stressed the dominance of Whig leadership. He virtually discounts a Liberal Party at all outside parliament until it was created from the 'bottom up' in the mid 1860s, and describes the parliamentary party before 1865 as "the expression of personal rivalries and political differences within the aristocracy, broadly defined".[23]

On the other hand Lord Blake, in his biography of Disraeli written at about the same time, suggests that the need for registration of voters brought about by the Great Reform Act meant that "the importance of party even in the 1830s and 1840s should not be underestimated".[24] Jonathan Parry, in his Rise and Fall of the Liberal Government, actually claims the existence of a Liberal Party from the 1830s, and one in which "Distinctions between 'Whigs'

---

20 Ian Newbould, *Whiggery and Reform 1830-41 The Politics of Government* (Basingstoke, 1990), pp.314-5.

21 Richard Brent, *Liberal Anglican Politics: Whiggery, Religion and Reform 1830-1841* (Oxford, 1987), p.63 and 'New Whigs In Old Bottles', *Parliamentary History*. II, pt.1 (1992), pp.151-156.

22 T A Jenkins, *The Liberal Ascendancy* 1830-1886 (London, 1994), pp.3/4.

23 John Vincent, *The Formation of the British Liberal Party 1857-68*. Penguin ed. (Harmondsworth, 1972), p.33.

24 Robert Blake, *Disraeli* (London, 1966), p.271.

and 'Radicals' were employed very loosely"[25] He talks of a parliamentary Whig-Liberal tradition and, while accepting that it lacked a professional national organisation, maintains that this alliance was central to British politics and founded on an able [Whig] parliamentary management of MPs.[26] Certainly the notion of 'party' in Whig eyes remained one centred on Parliament. The nature of Whiggism, indeed of mainstream Liberalism itself, accepted that political association was bound to be loose if there was also to be a commitment to rational argument and free debate, to the discovery of the 'right answer' through the power of reason and intellect rather than through 'organisation'. In hijacking control of the Reform Club from the Radicals, the Whigs not only took advantage of the latter's decline in parliamentary numbers, but sought to outflank electoral pressure groups through aiming primarily at the continued selection of the 'right sort' of men as members of parliament. Men who would control the pace of Reform to ensure that, if circumstances ultimately dictated further 'doses', the vote would go only to those who 'deserved' it. More importantly, that it would go only to those who could be trusted to oppose the real damage to Whig predominance of any change in the hugely inequitable distribution of seats in the House of Commons. Richard Cobden wrote in 1848 of the "entire powerlessness" of Dissenters among MPs and other independent Liberals. He went on to claim "that this must always be the case so long as the representation remains as it now is, giving to the landlords and parsons in the Counties and the aristocracy in little boroughs the power of returning 3/4ths of the members of the House."[27]

The large membership of the Reform Club was ideal for the recruitment of suitable parliamentary candidates from the increasingly politically aspirant professional and commercial middle classes. These could be encouraged to join, groomed as potential MPs under the supervision of the whips and influenced, even 'dazzled', by occasional acquaintanceship with the traditional political and social elite. Under the rules, those who might 'unfortunately' be adopted by local associations without the benefit of such prior induction could swiftly be placed at the head of candidates' lists for membership. Once elected they would be assimilated into the luxurious atmosphere, excellent cuisine, good company and, perhaps above all in Victorian Britain, status of London club life. The aim of the Whigs was to maintain a Whig-Liberal majority of MPs able to direct the expression of opinion in the country at large through the constitutional forum of Parliament, and able to persuade such opinion to accept the will of that Parliament. At the same time the Club also provided a headquarters from which the whips and party managers could co-ordinate the fighting of elections, and within which MPs were able to

25 Jonathan Parry, *The Rise and Fall of the Liberal Government in Victorian Britain* (Yale, 1993), pp.10 and 19.

26 Parry, *Rise and Fall of the Liberal Government.* p.10.

27 Richard Cobden to John Bright, 28 August 1848, CP, BL Add. mss. 43649, ff.71-2.

entertain supporters from their constituencies. Meanwhile the Whig grandees and their close associates could maintain their exclusivity at Brooks's, needing only to leave it from time to time to play the part of the politician at the Reform.

Professor Newbould has commented on the continued use of Brooks's by Whig leaders after the founding of the Reform Club. The parliamentary journalist and author, Henry Lucy, drew attention to the infrequency of Lord Granville's visits, while the Reform's hall porter is reported to have failed to recognise Lord Hartington on one occasion.[28] The Reform Club, for the first fifty years of its existence, is alleged never to have achieved quite the same balance of exclusiveness combined with catholicity of membership as the Carlton was able to do; a reflection perhaps of the more socially exclusive nature of the Whig as compared to Tory grandee. "...while the men at the head of the Conservative organisation use the Carlton Club daily, the club patronage of the Liberal chiefs is distributed over half-a-dozen clubs...The Whig or Liberal peer presumes upon the popularity of his political faith and thinks...he can indulge his social pride with impunity...The old Tories have years ago socially fused themselves in the new Conservatives. The Whigs have never fused themselves in the new Liberals..."[29] However, Dr Robert Farquharson MP, who joined both Brooks's and the Reform in the early 1880s, provides a reminder that not all aspirant club members of the middle classes were 'dazzled' by a social acquaintanceship with the Whiggish elite, however slight. He reminisces:

" I was told that it was necessary to belong to Brooks's, and my proposer told me that it would be prudent to conceal my connection with the medical profession, lest the suspicion of doing useful work in the world, outside politics, should outrage the delicate social susceptibility of my future associates...
I very soon made up my mind that it was not my line of country, to use a familiar phrase. I only sat there once, when I sat between two great Whig peers, who looked at me over their French novels and their champagne as though I belonged to a different species...My dinner cost me exactly double the amount I would have paid for it at the Reform.
Dining at the historical institution In St James's Street [Brooks's] has been compared with partaking of that meal in a nobleman's house with the host lying dead upstairs..."[30]

---

28 Newbould, *Whiggery and Reform*, p.196, H W Lucy, *A Diary Of The Salisbury Parliament 1886-1892* (London, 1892), p.200, Frederic Harrison, *Autobiographic Memoirs* (2 vols., London, 1911), Vol. II, p.81.

29 'A Liberal', 'The Social Discipline of the Liberal Party', *The Fortnightly Review*, XXXIII, New Series (June 1883), pp.768 and 773.

30 Right Hon. R Farquharson, *In and Out of Parliament - Reminiscences of a Varied Life* (London, 1911), p.90.

Nevertheless, the Whigs continued to dominate the political scene in the 1850s and 1860s, while Radicals failed to make any real impact after the success of their campaign to repeal the Corn Laws in 1846. Certainly the triumph of the Anti-Corn Law League prompted other Radical groups to start organising on a national basis. The earliest of these, the anti-State Church Association, which became the Liberation Society in 1853, formed a Dissenters' parliamentary committee in April 1847 under the chairmanship of Samuel Morley,[31] and was successful in defeating Whigs in such constituencies as Edinburgh, Bath, and Tower Hamlets. Some sixty MPs were alleged by this time to be pledged against endowment of religion by the State, with the 1850s witnessing a rise in parliamentary independence and fragmented politics.[32] But there is little doubt of the overall failure of parliamentary Liberals to maintain momentum in the cause of progressive policies, and this failure was linked to the Reform Club by Gladstone himself: "The Radical and independent Liberal party...is now practising...a deceit...for by standing before the country as primarily answerable for the feebleness and effeteness of parliamentary action, it will speedily lose the best part of whatever qualified hold it may have upon the public respect...He who turns from Pall Mall towards the Park between the Reform and Carlton Clubs will perceive that each of those stately fabrics is mirrored in the windows of the other..." No less an authority than Professor Matthew confirms the attribution of this article to Gladstone, claiming that it gives a clear and revealing account of his views about the proper development of British politics.[33] Interestingly Gladstone was still a member of the Carlton Club at this time. He did not resign until 1859, although it was reported that certain hot headed members had vowed that he ought to be pitched headlong out of the Club windows and through those of the Reform.[34]

In spite of anger and frustration at Whig arrogance and Whig exclusiveness, there was a fundamental recognition among the majority of anti-Conservatives that Whig leadership was still crucial to the return and maintenance of a Liberal government. The ability of Lord Palmerston to play on that recognition, his political shrewdness in 'smoothing ruffled feathers' by combining Whigs, Radicals and Peelites in his Cabinet of 1859, succeeded in 'toning down' Radicalism for another six years; that "lukewarm liberalism of the Palmerstonian era".[35] Many of those 'Palmerstonian Radicals' who allowed

---

31 Samuel Morley (1809-1886). Wealthy London hosier. Advanced Liberal and leading Nonconformist who sought partnership of capital and labour in industry and the election of working men to parliament. Major financial backer of the Reform League. Elected to the Reform Club in 1866 and an original member of its Political Committee.

32 D A Hamer, The Politics of Electoral Pressure: A Study In The History Of Victorian Reform Agitations (Harvester Press, 1977), p.94.

33 Anonymous (W E Gladstone), 'The Declining Efficiency of Parliament', Quarterly Review, XCIX (1856), pp.562 and 565. See also H C G Matthew, Gladstone 1809-74. Clarendon paperback ed. (Oxford. 1991), p.105.

34 W J Fisher, 'Liberal Clubs and the Liberal Party', Monthly Review, XVII (December 1904), pp. 128/9.

35 M Ostrogorski, Democracy and the Organisation of Political Parties (2 vols., London, 1902), Vol. 1, p.422.

themselves to be persuaded to tone down their Radicalism were members of the Reform Club. Some were to be counted among the members of its original Political Committee some ten years later. Perhaps their case was put best by the most obviously successful of their number, Thomas Milner Gibson: "...it is of no use to complain about governments being exclusive and being aristocratic if when they open the door you won't enter".[36] A comment, together with others of Milner Gibson at the time, which led to some mockery in The Times.[37]

Towards A Political Committee

The first recorded attempt at collective independent political action by members of the Reform Club had taken place in 1845. It seems likely in the light of its timing and the individual MPs involved that this was part of the climax to the campaign to repeal the Corn Laws. In February an unofficial committee of seven members of the Club recommended an examination of measures to improve the attendance of MPs at debates and divisions, and to promote the objects and principles (not detailed) of the Liberal Party.[38]

The political and social composition of the committee of seven was mixed, but on balance firmly Reformist and favoured repeal of the Corn Laws. There were two aristocratic Radicals, one of the principal parliamentary protagonists for repeal, Charles Villiers, and Chartist supporter Thomas Slingsby Duncombe. Ben Hawes, a wealthy soap manufacturer, and the Radical Henry Ward, were also both firm repealers. The remaining three were an Irish ex-Dragoon and free trader, David Ross: a Liberal lawyer in favour of shorter parliaments and the Ballot, Henry Tancred: and finally another lawyer, William Hayter, again a Corn Law repealer but Whiggish Liberal who became Lord John Russell's Chief Whip. The efforts of the committee of seven were endorsed by a further sixty-four members of the Club. No less than fifty-nine of these were MPs, although only five had ministerial experience and that at junior level. Most described themselves as Liberals or Reformers and ten as Radical Reformers, the majority drawn from the law and commerce, while six were Whigs or held themselves to be 'of Whig principles'. There is no record of any further action and the recommendations were not raised at the Annual General Meeting of that year. The Club's General Committee did not acknowledge the committee's existence, confining itself merely to recording

36 *The Times.* 27 *June 1859, p.12d.*

37 *The Times.* 28 *June 1859, p.9b. These 'Palmerstonian Radicals' included such future members of the Political Committee of the Reform Club as the wealthy Dissenters, Charles Gilpin and Francis Crossley; also Robert Dalgluish, W E Baxter, James Caird, H L E Bulwer, Robert Collier, James Stansfeld and, most notably, Charles Villiers and Thomas Milner Gibson. Most were lawyers or wealthy manufacturers given junior posts in the government and/or provided with baronetcies. Villiers and Milner Gibson were to join the Cabinet, in the latter case his friendship for Richard Cobden leading for a while to the 'muzzling' even of that famous Radical's critical faculties.*

38 *Reform Club mss., 17 February 1845, Box 9.*

agreement at the time to the use of the Blue Drawing Room as a meeting place for MPs, but only "at such times as may not interfere with the business of the Club".[39] Only five of the General Committee's thirty members are listed among the supporters of the committee of seven's recommendations. Lack of any further reference to the latter's activities no doubt reflected the return to party unity provided by the belated support of Lord John Russell for Repeal of the Corn Laws in his 'Edinburgh Letter' written in November 1845. The Act of Repeal itself was to follow within a year.

A second initiative was not taken for a further fifteen years, coinciding with the founding of the Liberal Registration Association in March 1860. The Association was part of an effort by the whips to counter the adoption of a more aggressive electoral policy adopted by the more progressive sections in the constituencies, while the initiative within the Club amounted to a proposal to form a political sub-committee to help with the co-ordination of parliamentary elections.[40] Consideration of the proposal was postponed to a Special General Meeting called for 31 May, ostensibly to allow members time for further thought. In the event only fifty-one members attended thus voiding the motion, a minimum of sixty being required by the rules for a vote to be taken.[41] Again it seems possible that a renewed sense of party unity, this time engendered by the formation of Lord Palmerston's second Ministry, may have overtaken the momentum to form such a sub-committee.

A third attempt from within the Reform Club to persuade its membership to play a more systematic and active political role followed within two years, initially taking the form of a one page circular dated 29 May 1862 and addressed 'For Members of the Club only'. The circular informed readers of the intention to form a 'Voluntary Association' to promote party unity and assist in the conduct of election petitions.[42] Little positive action followed immediately. However, the next year saw those attending a Special General Meeting on 11 June agree, by a majority of fifty-four to nineteen, on the formation of a committee to report on steps both to improve the mode of electing members to the Club, and on action which might be taken in order to further the interests of the Liberal Party.[43] In the remarkably short space of

---

39 *Reform Club, GC Minutes, 14 March 1845.*

40 Hamer, *Politics of Electoral Pressure. p.98. The formation of the Association by the whips amounted to a clear admission of the lack of organisation in constituencies. However, it never seems to have developed much beyond an information centre, no doubt due to lack of funds as well as resistance from progressive groups.*

41 *Reform Club, SGM Minutes, 31 May 1860.*

42 *Reform Club Circular dated 29 May 1862 contained inside the front cover of the minute book of the Electoral Council.*

43 *This committee was largely, but not exclusively, composed of 'Palmerstonian loyalists', mainly businessmen and lawyers, for example J H Brewer, G Wingrove Cooke and William Milbourne James. Among the seven other MPs were M T Bass, the wealthy brewer active in promoting trade unionism, Robert Crawford, an East Indian Company proprietor, Lord Fermoy, an Irish peer, Henry Danby Seymour, J P Brown Westhead, another wealthy merchant, and the pro-Palmerston but anti-Whig Independent, Ralph Bernal Osborne.*

two weeks the Committee of fifteen members, which included the Liberal Chief Whip, Henry Brand, had made its report.[44] The main recommendation, that the election of candidates to the Club should be placed in the hands of a Council of forty to be elected by the members as a whole, was also accompanied by a number of ringing declarations which drew attention to the political origins and role of the Club. These emphasised the political objects for which the Reform Club was instituted, and specifically encouraged the continued use of its rooms for political purposes "in order that the headquarters of the Liberal Party may be known and understood to be in the Reform Club". The Report went on to recommend the appointment of sub-committees "for the consideration of such subjects as may seem calculated to promote the political interests of the Club".[45]

The Electoral Council met on a number of occasions between June 1863 and April 1866 but a political sub-committee (of five members) was not formed until June 1864, and then only in the face of opposition on the spurious grounds that the Council had not been formed for that purpose.[46] However, in spite of those 'ringing declarations', there is again no record of any actual political action and the minutes of the Electoral Council make no further reference to its political sub-committee. The Council failed to last beyond 1866, its last meeting being recorded on 12 April of that year. Election to the Club by ballot was effectively reinstated at the Annual General Meeting of 3 May 1866. Although re-establishment of the Council was attempted at a Special General Meeting on 5 April 1867, it was voted down by a large majority with no record of the arguments deployed for or against.

This is not to suggest that the Club had no political role between 1836 and the formation of a Political Committee in 1869. There was such a role, but not an actively Reformist one. The whips used the Club to sound out the likely voting intentions of individual MPs. They also used it to gauge reactions in the important area of patronage, something Brand made clear in a letter to Gladstone on probable criticism from within the Club over a potential appointee to the Board of Inland Revenue.[47] There is also much evidence of provision from within the Club's membership of a 'pool' of aspiring parliamentary candidates to whom constituencies could turn when unable to find one of their own.[48] Groups of MPs undoubtedly used its

---

44 *Henry Bouverie Brand (1814-1892). Lord of the Treasury from 1855 to 1858 and Palmerston's Patronage Secretary/Chief Whip from 1859 to 1866. Elected to the Reform Club in 1858 and an original member of its Political Committee. Uniquely for an ex-whip he was elected Speaker of the House of Commons from 1872 to 1884, subsequently being created Viscount Hampden. Succeeded his brother as Baron Dacre in 1890.*

45 *Reform Club, EC Minute Book, See also copy of mss., 19 May 1863, Box 9.*

46 *Reform Club, EC Minutes, 2 June 1864.*

47 *Henry Brand to William Ewart Gladstone, 16 March 1867 and 24 March 1867, GP, BL Add. mss. 44194, ff.30, 35 and 36, Brand to Gladstone, 6 October 1862, BL Add. mss. 44193, f.61.*

48 *Philip Henry Bagenal, The Life of Ralph Bernal Osborne MP (London 1884), p.43, Alger Labouchere Thorold, The Life of Henry Labouchere (London, 1913), p.68, Gash, Politics in the Age of Peel. p.424, Ostrogorski, Democracy, p. 145.*

facilities for meetings among themselves and with representatives of constituency associations, this latter role one which the Earl of Durham had specifically envisaged in his plans for the Club in 1836.[49] Yet a majority of members seem to have been thoroughly lukewarm over the assumption inherent in the Club's title. A representative House of Commons and more equable share in the fruits of office may well have remained ideals of Liberalism as the Party entered the Gladstonian era, but such prizes continued to be perceived as the prerogative of the top half of society. Meaningful parliamentary democracy and Thomas Paine's <u>Rights Of Man</u> were not considered to 'stretch' beyond token elements of the 'deserving working class'. Meanwhile the caution with which mainstream middle class Liberals trod the path towards that still far distant democracy was reinforced among members of the Reform Club by an apparent inclination to place maintenance of the ethos of Club before the pursuit of active politics.

A cynic might claim with some justification that many members of the Reform Club were content with an absence of further Reform. Certainly, at least three major historians of the period have not 'pulled their punches' in commenting on the lack of Reforming zeal of many MPs who described themselves as Reformers.[50] More contemporaneously, the wealthy champion of the Trade Union Movement of the 1860s, Frederic Harrison, tells of a mass procession of Labour men through the streets in 1865 during the suffrage agitation of that year:

"As the procession passed [the Reform Club] with their banners, the men cheered the Club, taking it to be the seat of the Reforming Party. The habitues at the lower windows looked on, but did not reciprocate the compliment. We young Radicals above saluted the Unionists. And when a member of the Committee begged us to desist from showing sympathy with the men, we declined to share their contemptuous indifference to the workmen's salute."[51]

Even the agreeable and popular Charles Villiers, with a foot in both Radical and Whig camps, referred in 1860 to the anti-Reformers in the Reform Club,[52] while another contemporary perspective on all this is provided by Garibaldi's enormously popular visit to England in April 1864, which

---

49 Durham to Parkes, 20 March 1836, Reid, <u>Life And Letters Of The First Earl Of Durham</u>. Vol.II, p.80.

50 ". . . the ranks of MPs labelled 'Reformers' were full of men who never approved a major reform until their ministers presented it to them for approval." Southgate <u>Passing Of The Whigs.</u> p.78. See also Vincent, <u>Formation Of The British Liberal Party</u>. p.290 and Parry, <u>Rise and Fall of the Liberal Government</u>, p.12.

51 Harrison, <u>Autobiographic Memoirs</u>. Vol.II, p.80.

52 Charles Villiers to Lord John Russell, 14 June 1860, RP, PRO 30/22/25, f.382.

included being entertained to lunch 'in state' by the Reform Club. Garibaldi is reported to have commented on the strength of a practical freedom under the law in Britain, but understandably omitted to add how little that freedom embraced those other continental catch words of equality and fraternity.[53] It also has to be admitted that while some two hundred members of the Club put down a motion in favour, over forty objected to that invitation to lunch, a reflection no doubt of Garibaldi's revolutionary aura and of events in Europe since 1848. Continued lack of progress on further Reform was responsible for the outbreaks of disorderly public conduct organised by the predominantly working class Reform League In 1866 and 1867. The League was supported by a number of militant organisations, not least the First International, and the demonstrations organised on its behalf in Hyde Park in July 1866 and May 1867, together with the associated street processions and open air meetings in cities from London to Glasgow which followed the failure of Russell's Reform Bill in 1866, seem at last to have concentrated the political mind. For it can reasonably be argued that they played no small part in Parliament's belated acceptance of a Second, and this time Conservative, Reform Act in August 1867, with 'Hyde Park' now taking its place alongside 'Peterloo' as a second 'battle honour' of the working class.[54] Gladstone's first biographer, John Morley, was to comment:

"It is worthy of remark that not one of the main changes of that age was carried in parliament without severe agitation out of doors. Catholic emancipation was won by O'Connell; the Reform Act of 1832 by the political unions; free trade by the league against the corn law. Household suffrage [Second Reform Act] followed the same rule".[55]

Yet perhaps it would be wrong to judge too harshly those MPs who were members of the Reform Club in 1867. While many Liberals no doubt shared a "general reticence" on Reform, only eight of some forty-four Whig-Liberal 'Adullamites' who actually voted against their own government on Lord Dunkellin's rating amendment of 18 June 1866, thus effectively defeating the ageing Russell's final attempt to appease public opinion over Reform, were contemporary members of the Reform Club. [56]

53 *Manchester Guardian*, 18 April 1864. Garibaldi's statement is quoted at Steele, *Palmerston and Liberalism*, pp.230/1.

54 *For an account of the demonstrations in Hyde Park, and one view of their relationship to the Second Reform Act, see R Harrison, Before The Socialists Studies In Politics 1861-1881 (London, 1965), Chapter III.*

55 *John Morley, The Life of William Ewart Gladstone (3 vols., London, 1903), Vol II, p.227.*

56 *See Vincent, Formation of the British Liberal Party, pp.58 and 283. The eight were: Robert Lowe, appalled by the practice of popular politics in Australia and leader of the 'Adullamites', W B Beaumont, brother-in-law to Dunkellin, Colonel Biddulph, also a member of Brooks's, F Doulton who had personal reasons for voting against the government, W G Foster, J Mackie, M Marsh and J Goldsmid. The description 'Adullamite' was coined by John Bright, from 1 Samuel, Chapter 22: David gathered unto him at the cave of Adullam "everyone that was in distress...and everyone that was discontented..."!*

2 FORMATION OF THE POLITICAL COMMITTEE

Composition And Role

The eventual formation of the Political Committee of the Reform Club should be seen against a background of efforts to encourage the unity of party from the centre in the wake of the Reform Act of 1867. Several references to the potential loss of seats from competing Liberal candidates can be found in the correspondence of George Glyn, Gladstone's new Chief Whip, during the run-up to the general election of 1868.[57] Added to these are complaints about the absence of the usual financial support from the Party's grandees.[58] Yet belated agreement by the Club in 1869 to such a committee came too late. The 1870s finally saw the expansion of representative constituency power as the major collective force for the encouragement of party political unity. This left the apparently anachronistic committee of a metropolitan club, widely if perhaps unfairly perceived as exclusive, concerned with trying to justify such actions as it did take to the point of having to defend its existence within the Club itself. The days of an inherited tradition of political power were dying, at least in the Liberal Party, although it was not until 1886 that the last rites were said over the corpse. By 1869 men had already "sensed the beginnings of a new dispensation", even if the organising ability of Joseph Chamberlain was not yet a major factor.[59] Perhaps all this is to make a lot of not very much, as policy and priorities for legislation were by then securely in the hands of the Executive, a situation to be consolidated during the prolonged 'reign' of Gladstone. His particular political strength as the focus of a more broadly based Liberalism was based on popular appeal to the individual voter, and owed little to the organisation of party. Where policy was involved he concerned himself hardly at all with the lobbying of parliamentary support. "Gladstone's inclination was always to proceed by written argument. . . The development of policy by social intercourse was not Gladstone's method: in the whole of his first premiership he does not record entering a political club".[60] By 1869 at least nine-tenths of legislation was passing through the hands of the government.

---

57 George Grenfell Glyn (1824-1887). Partner in the banking firm of Glyn, Mills and Co. The first Liberal Chief Whip appointed (by Gladstone) from outside the traditional Whiggish elite. He retained the appointment until 1873, when he succeeded his father as (2nd) Baron Wolverton. Elected to the Reform Club in 1862 and one of the original members of its Political Committee.

58 George Glyn to Gladstone, 4 and 22 September, 3 and 8 October and 14 November 1868, GP, BL Add. mss. 44347, ff.151, 176, 188, 191 and 244.

59 Southgate, Passing Of The Whigs, p.337. Joseph Chamberlain (1836-1914) was elected Mayor of Birmingham in 1873 and to Parliament in 1876. Founder of the National Liberal Federation (Caucus) formed in 1877 after failure to establish a separate Radical party. Entered the Cabinet in Gladstone's Second Administration in 1880, but opposed to him on Home Rule and joined Lord Salisbury's 'Conservative and Unionist' Cabinet in 1895. Elected to the Reform Club in 1877 and resigned over the blackballing of his two brothers in 1882.

60 Matthew, Gladstone 1809-1874, p.233.

Now leader of the Party and Prime Minister, Gladstone was invited to join the Reform Club in the Spring of 1869 under a new rule which permitted the General Committee to invite two members annually without having their names submitted to a ballot. It seems he was not impressed by the invitation and in particular having to pay a membership fee! In a letter of 19 May Glyn urged him to join. "I thought the invitation was to you as an 'honorary member'. . . They will feel hurt if you do not accept. . . Granville has accepted in terms that selection to such a Club is the desire of his heart!!. . . Please accept. . . of course you would not use the Club". Within this letter Glyn makes the first reference to a Political Committee. He draws Gladstone's attention to the Club's reorganisation as a political body "trying under your banner to unite both sections". He goes on to say that in this respect "it is different from Brooks (sic)", a comment which makes clear that the lack of unity to which he refers was that between those Liberals of a Whiggish tendency and the Radical elements of the Party.[61] For it should be emphasised that in 1869 there were still no members of trade societies or unions, no artisans, no representatives of the 'aristocracy of labour' among members of the Reform Club. It was to be another twelve years before the Club elected its first member from the ranks of organised labour. Interestingly this was achieved under the terms of that same rule which had seen Gladstone avoid the ballot in the case of his own membership.

Nevertheless, the nature of public political debate itself was seen to be changed with the growth of manufacturing and Nonconformist influence and wealth, the expansion of the provincial Press, great strides in literacy, and the proliferation of working class clubs and trade associations. "Politics for more than twenty years after the 1867 Reform Act became the central preoccupation of the nation".[62] Yet it is an indication of the failure of Liberals to grasp the significance of the changes brought about by the Second Reform Act, in particular the increase in the working class vote in the boroughs, that attempts to reinforce the structure of party were largely confined to tinkering with the title and organisation of the headquarters of the Registration Association, and to forming a Political Committee of the Reform Club. Members of the Club voted to establish the latter at their annual general meeting on 6 May 1869. Appropriately the motion was proposed and seconded respectively by two MPs both firm, even typical, supporters of Gladstone, J P Brown Westhead and J A Hardcastle. The former was a wealthy Mancunian merchant with a keen interest in the promotion of partnership between capital and labour, and the latter a Suffolk lawyer closely

---

61 *Glyn to Gladstone, 19 May 1869, GP, BL Add. mss. 44347, ff.294-6. One of Gladstone's early actions on resigning the leadership of the Liberal Party in 1875 was to give up his membership of the Reform Club, although he continued to attend major social occasions at the Club as an honoured guest.*

62 H J Hanham, <u>Elections And Party Management: Politics In The Time Of Disraeli And Gladstone,</u> *Harvester Press ed. (Sussex, 1978), p.xi.*

associated with the Liberal whips. Members agreed that the Club's Rule XIV should provide for a Committee on the following lines:

"The political affairs of the Club shall be managed by a Committee of fifty members, who shall be elected by ballot at the same time as the General Committee, and under the supervision of the same Scrutineers, the majority of whom shall deliver to the Secretary, at the close of the ballot, a list, signed by themselves, of the names of those who have the greatest number of votes, and in case of equality of votes, the majority of Scrutineers shall then decide, and the list so formed shall be the Political Committee for the year. Ten members of the Committee shall retire annually, being eligible however for re-election, and fifteen shall form a quorum. The Political Committee shall, at its first meeting after each election, appoint a Sub-Committee from among its Members, delegating such powers as may be deemed necessary."[63]

In the light of members' wishes that election was to be by ballot, the composition of that first Committee suggests that the political complexion of the Club as a whole in 1869 was overwhelmingly 'Gladstonian'. An annotated list of the fifty members elected from a total candidature of ninety-six is attached at Appendix 2. It is not surprising to find Gladstone's Chief Whip at the head of the poll, with his predecessor in that appointment in second place. It provides confirmation of the important place held by the whips within the Club. Further analysis provides the following additional information. No less than forty of the fifty were MPs. Eighteen were barristers, four solicitors, and fourteen were manufacturers or merchants. At least nine were Dissenters, the majority of these being Radicals and/or 'in trade'. Twenty-one were 'mainstream Liberal' or Irish Liberal MPs, virtually all of whom could be counted on as supporters of Gladstone. A further eleven were among that group of Radical MPs who had moderated their Radicalism during Palmerston's Second Administration. These could now largely be counted upon as ministerialist in fact or by nature, and thus also supporters of the new Liberal government. Only four were 'independent' Radicals and another four of Whiggish sympathy. The final ten, those who were not MPs, included such 'loyal party men' as Richard Baxter, W G Beare, W D Cooper, Charles de la Pryme, and W Fraser Rae. A large majority were over fifty years old in 1869 and at least fourteen over sixty. The various groupings under which the fifty have been listed in the Appendix are an admittedly subjective interpretation of their political affiliations. Some might well be said to have had a 'foot in more than one camp'. For example, John Locke was an associate in the late 1850s of M T Bass and William Jackson. Villiers and Milner Gibson, although undeniably Radicals, might equally well be said to have had Whiggish tendencies, while William Cogan and John Esmonde were

63 Reform Club, PC Minute Book 1, p.3. At the Club's AGM the following year on 5 May 1870 it was agreed that the numbers necessary to provide a quorum should be reduced to seven.

frequently accused of being Whigs by the more militant supporters of Home Rule among their Irish colleagues. Yet the impression is one of an overwhelming majority cautious in the pursuit of Reform and not over enthusiastic about other than a very limited extension of the franchise. Twenty-four members attended the first meeting on Monday 14 June 1869, a figure, it has to be admitted, seldom to be reached again. Brown Westhead was elected Chairman and, subsequently, James Caird and William Cogan as Vice-Chairmen and representatives respectively of Scottish and Irish Liberal interests. On 21 June, in accordance with its terms of reference, the Committee elected a sub-committee of eleven, of whom it was decided that three should be sufficient for a quorum.

Little more of note occurred until early 1870, no doubt due to the absence of members of the full Committee from London during the parliamentary recess. Numbers present at meetings called in July, November and December 1869 rarely made up a quorum. It was not until the following May that the Political Committee felt able to forward the following proposals for its functions to the General Committee for their approval:

"To promote the political organisation of the Liberal Party, and to aid the several constituencies in securing suitable candidates for seats.
To arbitrate between conflicting Liberal candidates at Parliamentary Elections contesting the same seat or seats, in order to prevent the loss of seats by division in the Liberal ranks.
To suggest and carry out such changes in the rules and regulations of the Club as may from time to time be found necessary to secure its useful political action."

Two further functions were proposed by members but for the time being these were discarded. One concerned the setting up of a political fund, but this was deemed inexpedient under present circumstances. The other proposed powers similar to those of the General Committee, to enable the Political Committee to bypass the ballot and elect five members annually to the Club who would be "likely to promote the general interests of the Liberal Party".[64]

The first of the three approved functions effectively formalised an existing ad hoc practice. The second was to lead the Committee into much controversy, but placed a finger squarely on the Party's major difficulty in the constituencies. The third, while provoking some division within the Committee, was to lead to little positive action. Of the two functions which did not see the light of day on this occasion, it is difficult to say why that relating to a political fund should have been discarded. Support from the Party's grandees had been severely reduced and Glyn's problems at the general election would have been fresh in his mind. It may be that the Committee anticipated aversion among members to the Club being used as a

64 Reform Club, PC Minute Book 1, p.55.

'collective' instrument for political fund ratings. Private subscriptions via the whips or direct to candidates were after all the norm. However, it was eventually agreed that open subscription lists should be placed in the public rooms before general elections, this being done in 1880, 1885 and 1886; in 1886, it must be added leading to considerable embarrassment and ultimately the posting of two lists, including a separate one for Liberal Unionists. The proposal to permit the Committee to elect members directly to the Club was resurrected later, leading in 1877 to an amended rule IV which delegated an element of the existing authority of the General Committee on this issue to the Political Committee. This new rule IV laid down that individuals so elected by the Political Committee must have "proved their attachment to the Liberal cause by marked and obvious services. . ." Additionally such elections were to be restricted to just two individuals annually from the candidates' book. The Committee was required to sit in special session for the purpose with at least ten members present, and to reach an unanimous vote. One understandable proviso was that no candidate previously blackballed could be elected in this way.

Between 1869 and 1886, its politically active period, the Political Committee was to meet once or twice a month when Parliament was in session, an average at that time of some seven or eight meetings a year although the number tended to increase during years in which general elections were held. The Committee made much use of Rule IV, even after 1886 when unanimity was reached by settling apparently on a policy of electing one Liberal Unionist and one supporter of Home Rule on each occasion. The first 'working class' members of parliament, Thomas Burt and Henry Broadhurst, were elected to the Reform Club under Rule IV in respectively 1880 and 1882. A number of editors of influential national and regional newspapers were also early nominees for membership under the Rule, an indication that the Committee was fully aware of the power of the Press. These included Stoddart of the Glasgow Herald in 1877, Dunckley of the Manchester Examiner in 1878, Lloyd of the Daily Chronicle and Cooper of the Scotsman in 1881, and Lucy of the Daily News in 1885. Edward Dicey, editor of the Observer, was alone among invited editors in declining the honour (1886). He did so on the grounds that acceptance of nomination by the Political Committee would compel him "either to curtail full liberty of comment and criticism or to give offence to a body of men whose good opinion I highly value".[65]

Lost Opportunities

The Gladstonian Liberal Party entered the new parliamentary session of 1870 with two central organisations concerned with the maintenance of a unified party structure, the Liberal Registration Association and the Political

---

65 *Reform Club, PC Minute Book 3, p.26. Edward Dicey was an imperialist, being a forceful advocate of the annexation of Egypt in the early 1880s. He believed that the foreign policy of Gladstone's 2nd Administration (1880-1885) had seriously undermined Britain's status in the world.*

Committee of the Reform Club, neither exactly influential at constituency level. Regrettably the early minutes of the Liberal Central Association, which by 1874 had been formed by integrating the London office of the Liberal Registration Association with the Whips' Office into a form of 'party headquarters', are missing.[66] Meanwhile the early minutes of the Political Committee of the Reform Club contain no direct reference to Nonconformist anger over Clause 25 of the Elementary Education Act of 1870. Neither do they refer to the fury of Liberal temperance supporters within the UK Alliance at the regulation of public houses through the Licensing Act of 1872. They provide no hint either of the betrayal felt by organised labour at the Administration's failure to clarify the law on strikes and confirm the right to picket in the Trades Union and Criminal Law Amendment Acts of 1871.[67] By 1873 the Liberal leadership had angered many of its Nonconformist, temperance and trade union supporters, in spite of a successful programme of other major reforms including the reorganisation of the Army, the introduction of a competitive entry for the Civil Service, the opening of universities to Nonconformists, and a comprehensive modernisation of the judicial system. Further, with the effective formation of an Irish Home Rule Party between 1871 and 1873, it had lost the 'guarantee' of parliamentary support from the bulk of its Irish membership. Mainstream Gladstonian Liberals were shaken by the doubts thrown on the government's probity by its fiscal mismanagement in 1873. They also shared the concern of the Whigs at the growing profile of working class Radicalism. Between 1871 and Disraeli's victory at the general election of February 1874, the Conservatives gained twenty-eight seats from thirty-two by-elections.

Without suggesting the presence of a potential revolutionary situation in the early 1870s, the political establishment, of which the Reform Club must be considered a part, is not likely to have forgotten the disorders in major cities during 1866 and 1867 and, in particular, those at Hyde Park. The fall of Napoleon III in September 1870, establishment of the Paris Commune of 1871 and the demonstration in London in its support on 16 April at a time of increasing public disenchantment with the monarchy, would also have concentrated minds. An effort was made from within the Political Committee to rebuild bridges between the Party and organised labour through the newly formed Labour Representation League (LRL).[68] Election to the Committee in May 1870 of the militant Nonconformist Radical, Edward Jenkins, was

---

66 *The minute book is part of a set of four covering the period up to 1914, at one time part of the Gladstone Library of the National Liberal Club. The remaining three minute books (1883 to 1914) are now held within the Special Collections Department of the University of Bristol, as are most of the other contents of the Gladstone Library.*

67 *Regulation of public houses under the Licensing Act accepted their right to exist and thus tacitly their 'respectability'. Clause 25 of the Elementary Education Act permitted the new local, often sectarian, education boards to subsidise Anglican schools at the expense of all ratepayers.*

68 *The LRL was formed in 1869 as an effective successor to the Reform League. Its original primary aim was to obtain the election of working men to Parliament. However, during the 1870s it was largely incorporated into the Trades Union Congress, an organisation which concentrated then on pressure for legislation to improve the working conditions of its members rather than seeking an independent Labour political platform.*

followed by those of other able supporters of the right for equal treatment under the law for employees.[69] Sir David Wedderburn was elected in 1871, A J Mundella in 1874, Sir Charles Dilke in 1875, Professor Leonard Courtney in 1878, and Peter Rylands in 1879, joining such supporters of the partnership between capital and labour as Samuel Morley and M T Bass. Jenkins lost no time in arranging a meeting with representatives of the LRL. A resolution agreeing to co-operation with the League through a sub-committee, which included both Henry Brand and George Glyn, was recorded two weeks later. An extract from the sub-committee's report on the adoption of parliamentary candidates from the working class, put to the full Committee at a meeting on 2 May 1871, is set out below. It provides a flavour of the divisions within society at the time. It also reflects the views of perhaps more far sighted Liberals struggling without much success to overcome inertia within the Party, an inertia reflected in both Club and Political Committee. Equally, an apparent failure to act on the Report confirms the continued presence of a cautious approach among most members towards the encouragement of a more broadly based Legislature, a caution it must be added shared by Gladstone himself:

"We believe that it would be for the Public Good and would improve our Representative System if the Working Classes were directly represented in Parliament by intelligent Members of their own body taking their due share in the work of Legislation. And with that view your Sub Committee have been in friendly communication with leading Members of the Working Classes. We have assured them of our loyal cooperation and we strongly recommend this important subject to the constant attention of the Political Committee with a view to effect the object as opportunities may arise."[70]

No vote on this recommendation, indeed no response at all from the full Committee, is recorded at a time when the current of progressive Liberal thinking and of political foresight in the wake of the Second Reform Act could be said to have favoured integrating working men fully into the Liberal Party. Clearly organised labour remained just another pressure or interest group to mainstream Liberals notwithstanding revolutionary developments on the Continent. There is no record of any effort on the part of the Political Committee to use its influence in those areas which might have given practical effect to the primary aim of the League at the time, and indeed to the wishes of its own sub-committee. For example these would have included

---

69 *Edward Jenkins* (1838-1884). *Barrister and author. Entered Parliament as member for Dundee in 1874 having split the anti-Conservative vote in previous by-elections there, and at Truro in 1871, thus letting a Conservative in on these occasions. Member of National Education League and a Trustee of the National Agricultural Labourers' Union. Variously described as 'a violent and semi-independent Radical, presumptuous and self conceited'. Described himself as an 'Advanced Liberal'. Elected to the Reform Club in 1867 and a member of its Political Committee from 1870 to his death in 1884.*

70 *Reform Club, PC Minute Book 1, pp. 76/7.*

a reduction in the high cost of a parliamentary candidate's deposit, the introduction of an element of public funding towards his election expenses, and the preparation of a list of appropriate constituencies which might be fought by Liberal Party sponsored candidates from the Labour Movement. Indeed the Committee, as part of a discussion on the Ballot Bill, voted on 2 May 1871 against a recommendation in favour of the payment of candidates' expenses out of imperial funds.[71] It may be that the majority were relying on inclusion in the Bill of a clause recommending their payment out of local rates, but such a clause (18) was defeated heavily in the Commons with a number of Liberals from across the Party voting with the Conservatives. One month later, on 6 June, members also baulked at a motion for a deputation to wait upon the Prime Minister to urge their collective view on the Bill. Members are on record as preferring to pass a resolution re-assuring themselves that the government was "pushing it [Ballot Bill] forward in the most effective manner."[72] There was much anxiety in June among Radicals on the progress of the Ballot Bill, which had already been delayed for a year. There were fears that the government's concentration on Cardwell's reorganisation of the Army would result in the Bill failing to complete all its stages by the end of the session; and these fears proved justified.[73]

It has been alleged that the cause of direct representation was not strongly supported by the majority of the working classes.[74] Nevertheless, the election of Thomas Burt for Morpeth in 1874 shows clearly the level of working class support which could be mobilised by the ranks of organised labour if the will to do so was present.[75] Suspicion remains that middle class reluctance to be represented by a working class MP, combined with a lack of funds for electoral expenses and for the maintenance of an MP once at Westminster, remained the main reason for the lack of working class candidates, rather than any preference on the part of the ranks of organised labour for middle class MPs. The Liberal Central Association and the whips had little money to spare whatever their views on the suitability of individuals. As the fundamental disunity of the Liberal Party re-asserted itself, as public perception of Gladstone's Administration altered with legislation which failed

---

71 *Reform Club, PC Minute Book 1, p. 74.*

72 *Reform Club, PC Minute Book 1, pp.83/4.*

73 *The Lords effectively rejected a much shortened Bill in the second week of August on the somewhat spurious grounds of the lateness of the session precluding its proper examination. Reintroduced the following year the Ballot Bill eventually received the Royal Assent on 18 July 1872, but election expenses continued to be borne by candidates.*

74 *Eugenio F Biagini,* Liberty, Retrenchment And Reform: Popular Liberalism in the Age of Gladstone 1860-1880 *(Cambridge, 1992), pp.342 including note 200, and 345. Biagini lists thirteen working class candidates in 1874 of whom only two, including Burt, were elected. Between 1874 and 1906 only twenty-four were elected.*

75 Thomas Burt *(1837-1922). Secretary of the 'Union' of Northumberland Miners from 1865 to 1913. Stood as a Radical for Parliament but remained a loyal supporter of Gladstone and Irish Home Rule. Retired in 1918 as 'Father of the House'. Elected to the Reform Club by the Political Committee under Rule IV in 1880, having turned down an invitation in 1879, and elected a member of that Committee in 1883.*

to meet the expectations of many of its rank and file supporters, so the Liberal Central Association and the Political Committee remained associated with continued Whig domination of the Party. There is no doubt of a continuing perception of the exclusive nature of the Reform Club in the public eye, of its metropolitan and Whig 'taint' in an era of rapidly expanding local constituency confidence against the background of the broader franchise supplied by the Reform Act of 1867. This was a taint which could even spill over into furious condemnation of such Radical standard bearers as John Bright. That not altogether fair, if perhaps understandable, view is summed up by the following extract from a letter in an admittedly militant Radical newspaper during the general election campaign of 1868. It was written primarily in the context of the support by Bright for Alexander Brogden's candidature in the newly created working class borough of Wednesbury. Brogden, a member, was allegedly 'sponsored' by the Reform Club of which the author accused Bright later in the article of being the 'Jupiter tonans'! It was headed 'Political Iscariots - Bright and Bribery' and signed 'Gracchus':

"Let the working classes be assured that the Reform Club which has deluged the country with electoral candidates destitute of all political principle, but possessed with weighty money-bags, has but one object in view, and that is the recovery of place, power and patronage. The Reform Club has done more to shut out working men from Parliament than the Tory Carlton. Wherever a working man has presented himself to a working class constituency he has been met with the rattle of whig money-bags in his face..."[76]

Such comments can be selected from a variety of sources, for example an angry attack by Joseph Chamberlain in 1873 on the Liberal leadership. Citing a "glorious inactivity" in the direction of Liberal politics, he links together three agencies as the responsible 'partners in crime': the authority of the treasury whip, the "want of definiteness" in official Liberal parliamentary candidates, and the Political Committee of the Reform Club. In August 1878 The Times published a letter from a Mr George Hough which described the political influence of London clubs as close to that of rotten boroughs: ". . . it has served the purpose of keeping political power in the hands of the few while the form of liberty has been given to the many." In 1882 the highly respected Spectator referred to the potential folly of any "explosion of caste-feeling" in the Reform Club when reporting the blackballing of Joseph Chamberlain's brothers that year.[77] Hostile press comment followed the Political Committee on most occasions when it sought to arbitrate between

76 <u>Reynolds Newspaper,</u> 1 November 1868 and quoted at H J Hanham, 'British Party Finance 1868-80', <u>Bulletin of the Institute of Historical Research,</u> XXVII (1954), p.78.

77 J Chamberlain, 'The Liberal Party and its Leaders', <u>Fortnightly Review,</u> XIV, New Series (September 1873), pp.288 and 300, <u>The Times,</u> 22 August 1878, p.6c, <u>Spectator.</u> 20 May 1882, p.649. The dispute over the Chamberlain affair is covered more fully later.

competing Liberal candidates. It dogged their footsteps over explusions from the Club in the case of individuals found guilty of 'political deviation'. Yet paradoxically, or perhaps consequentially if this perceived exclusivity had some foundation in reality, the length of the Club's waiting list showed the desirability of membership. Indeed the popularity of the political clubs of London had never been higher as literally hundreds queued for the privilege of joining the Reform. The City Liberal Club was founded in 1874 to cater for bankers and other men of the City of London, and the Devonshire Club in 1875 specifically to provide for the Reform's 'overflow'.[78]

There is no doubt that Radicals failed to dominate within the Political Committee during the early years of its existence. This reflected their position as a minority within the Club. It may also have contributed to the frustration and disappointment of much of the rank and file of the new Gladstonian Liberal Party in the constituencies, including representatives of organised labour. The Reform Act of 1867 set in train an irreversible movement towards democracy, however slow its initial progress. It could be argued that the newly formed Political Committee of the Reform Club should have been in the van of that movement rather than part of the process by which it was slowed down. But all this is to judge with hindsight. In the Committee's defence, its position was one perfectly consistent with loyalty to Gladstone, and the balance he sought to maintain between the increasingly strident demands of a burgeoning democracy and the need to retain the principle of tried and tested Whig leadership of a broadly based Party. Equally, there is no doubt that the Reform Club and its Political Committee were perceived from outside the Club's walls, understandably and in spite of its largely commercial and professional middle class membership, as being too much in the pocket of traditional influences.

Radical Disillusionment

In the wake of the disastrous result for the Liberals of the general election of 1874 including the effective destruction of Roman Catholic Liberalism as a political force in Ireland, Edward Jenkins made yet another attempt to persuade the Political Committee of the need for active involvement in the Party's organisation. He proposed that a delegation should wait upon Liberal leaders to discuss how the Committee might be used to this end.[79] On 21 June, presumably with the backing of Party leaders, members voted in favour

---

78 *The Reform Club's Annual Report of 21 April 1874 noted that the number of candidates awaiting admission was greater than at any time since its formation. The name 'Devonshire' provides a clue to the continuing predominance of Whigs at the heart of Liberal clubland as well as at the head of the Party. The Marquis of Hartington, heir to the dukedom, became the Club's first chairman with the Duke himself its first President. A membership of 1100 was reached in the first year as Liberals sought to rebuild their morale after defeat in the general election of 1874.*

79 *Reform Club, PC Minute Book 1, p.102.*

of closer ties with the new Liberal Central Association.[80] Clearly the Committee felt that it should at least place its relationship with the Association and whips on a more formal basis, Glyn having succeeded to the peerage on the death of his father, the first Lord Wolverton, the previous July. By mid 1875 the new Liberal Chief Whip, William Adam, had offered to nominate selected members of the Political Committee to seats on the Executive Committee of the Association.[81] In July Charles Villiers, and two other members of the original Committee, Lewis Morris and A W Young, together with a new member, Sir Charles Dilke, were elected by ballot to fill four such seats, the last named in particular providing an influential Radical presence at the organising heart of the Party.[82] In return the Political Committee agreed to re-open the issue of a political fund, proposing that money raised by voluntary subscription from Club members to this end should be divided between the Association and the Chief Whips' own election fund.[83] Both Adam, and Lord Kensington, also from the whips' office, were elected to the Committee in May 1876, thus restoring the close link with the Association which had been present before Glyn's succession to the peerage. Yet such measures promoted from the centre can hardly be said to have achieved much towards advancing the cause of Reform or that of democracy within the Party. They merely served to bind the Committee more closely to a Liberal leadership which, following Gladstone's formal resignation in January 1875, had further consolidated Whig power being headed now by Earl Granville and the Marquis of Hartington. Radicals were soon to turn their attention to the level of the constituency and attempt to fashion both democracy and a unified party from the 'bottom up'.

The frustrated efforts of Radicals such as Edward Jenkins to promote the cause of Radicalism through the central machinery of the Liberal Party, following defeat at the general election of 1874, reflect the lack of success among Radicals within the House of Commons in organising themselves as a collective political force. Even Dilke, who was appointed Chairman of the Liberal Central Association in 1876, failed to make a real impact on the Party's organisation. However it is true that, by this time, he was attempting to establish a more 'respectable' image after his earlier independent, not to

---

80 *Reform Club, PC Minute Book 1, p.108*. This is the first reference of the change in name of the Liberal Registration Association to Liberal Central Association.

81 <u>William Patrick Adam</u> *(1823-1881). Barrister. Scottish whip 1865 to 1873. Liberal Chief Whip while the Party was in Opposition from 1874 until he was appointed Governor of Madras following success at the general election of 1880. Elected to the Reform Club in 1866 and a member of its Political Committee from 1876 to 1880.*

82 <u>Sir Charles Dilke</u> *(1843-1911). Radical leader and member of Gladstone's Cabinet from December 1882 to June 1885, the year the scandal of Donald Crawford's divorce ended Dilke's brilliant career. He was elected to the Reform Club in 1867 and a member of its Political Committee from 1875 to 1885.*

83 *Reform Club, PC Minute Book 1, pp.118-121.*

say republician, Radical stance. By 1878 not only Dilke, but also Joseph Chamberlain, the latter an MP for only two years, had given up their attempt to rally Radicals in Parliament under the banner of a 'New Party'. Chamberlain had even 'flirted' temporarily with the 'Irish Home Rulers' until put off by Parnell's obstructive tactics in the House of Commons.[84] He now changed his strategy, seeking to unify and thus maximise Liberal voting strength in the constituencies through a national broad based party organisation, rather than by the traditional Radical method of local or sectionalist groups. Thus the creation of a National Liberal Federation (NLF) in 1877, launched with the active help of the 'temporarily retired' Gladstone, and designed to provide a vehicle for the reform of party and policy from the grassroots. This was the 'marriage' of civic leadership, composed of a new breed of second generation well educated and successful businessmen, with the enlarged electorate of the fast growing urban constituencies. It was a union through which 'control' of the process of selection of large numbers of parliamentary candidates could be wrested from the largely landed political hierarchy, and through which the responsiveness of MPs to constituents once in office might be improved. One of its direct consequences was to increase the need for arbitration between competing Liberal candidates, with the leadership itself compelled to take a hand during the general election of 1880 through boards of arbitration.[85]

In 1878, just one year after the formation of the NLF and less than ten after the founding of the Political Committee, one of the latter's more prominent members, W Fraser Rae, wrote an article in which he sought to clarify the political role of the Reform Club. Claiming that in the early years of the Club's existence members had played an active role in managing elections, Rae went on to maintain that this erstwhile level of political influence had now rightly diminished "because of local independence". He added that the Political Committee "never interferes in the conduct of elections, unless at the special request of the parties concerned, and then only with a view to smooth over differences and to act as a court of conciliation. . . the insidious manner in which the Reform Club is said by the imaginative correspondents of country newspapers to thwart one candidate or help another is pure fiction. . . The only body acting on behalf of the Liberal Party as a whole is the Liberal Central Association, established in 1860". Much of

---

84 Recruits for the 'New Party' during 1876 were few. In addition to Chamberlain and Dilke they included Joseph Cowen, Thomas Burt, L L Dilwyn, E D Gray and John Morley. See Thomas William Heyck, <u>The Dimensions of British Radicalism: The Case of Ireland (1874-95)</u> (Illinois, 1974), p.11, including note 12, and Peter Marsh, <u>Joseph Chamberlain Entrepreneur In Politics</u> (Yale, 1994), pp.113, 115 and 121.

85 The NLF aspired to put the management of the Party into the hands of a Federation of Liberal Constituency Associations each made up of representative committees appointed by elected committees of party members from each of the wards of a constituency. Likened to the 'Caucus' within the machinery of politics in the United States by those opposed to it, the NLF was effectively to amalgamate with the Liberal Central Association in 1887, deserting Chamberlain and remaining loyal to Gladstone following the split in the Party over Home Rule in 1886.

Rae's article was devoted to denying the need for too great a concentration by Liberals on organisation. He was particularly critical of the development of the newly formed NLF. He described it as an "ingenious method for obtaining a mechanical majority", at the same time warning of the dangers of a party political governing body in which there is no opposition, and of the "tyranny which is the essence of the system when fully developed". Rae was at pains to stress that in his view the nation's Constitution should be untrammelled alike by party clubs and political associations. "Unity is vital to political success but unity among Liberals can only be found through persuasion"; a sentiment with which no Whig could possibly have quarrelled.[86]

Rae's views are significant in the context of the Political Committee of the Reform Club. They confirm a clear cut difference of opinion between an apparent minority of largely Radical activists and many mainstream Liberals about the role of the Club, even if this is rarely obvious from the Political Committee's minutes. An original member and its elected Honorary Secretary for sixteen years from 1871 until his resignation in 1887, Rae attended more meetings than any other member. He was also Chairman of the Club's Library Committee from 1873 until his death in 1905, the library being a notable centre for political research during his chairmanship, and he had been a correspondent for a major Liberal daily newspaper, the Daily News. Rae's views seem likely to have reflected those of the majority in both Club and Political Committee alike, but one of the stated functions of the latter did include 'arbitration' between conflicting Liberal candidates at parliamentary elections. Arbitration suggests the existence of a more judgmental role than Rae's 'court of conciliation', and this 'wooliness' of perception was to lead to some difficulty during an era of increasing local electoral consciousness, particularly in the all important boroughs.

Radical hopes of a Liberal club as a focus for constituency associations of the National Liberal Federation, and one therefore at the heart of reforming politics, were not altogether abandoned. It is no accident that the concept of a National Liberal Club should have been raised in the early 1880s. That Club was established in November 1882 with a large membership of some three and a half thousand. A temporary clubhouse was opened (by Gladstone) in May 1883. The National Liberal Club has been described by the author of its only published history as "a really serious endeavour to find a home for democracy, void of the class distinctions associated with the

---

86 W Fraser Rae, 'Political Clubs and Party Organisation', Nineteenth Century, III (May 1878), pp.919 and 921-931.

Devonshire and the Reform Clubs".[87] Christopher Harvie in his Lights of Liberalism claims that the National Liberal Club owed its parentage to the Radical Club,[88] and Ostrogorski links the loss of an "active political spirit" on the part of the Reform Club directly with the founding of the National Liberal Club. He comments:

> "Consequently "to infuse new blood" into Liberalism. . . a new general centre for the party was founded in London in 1882, under the name of the National Liberal Club, intended. . . to serve as the great exchange of the Liberal Party, in which information and impressions as to the condition of Liberalism in the country would pass between the members. . . "[89]

The National Liberal Club was to react differently to other Liberal clubs over the issue of Home Rule for Ireland in 1886. Within three years it had shed most of its Liberal Unionist membership, a reflection perhaps of its closer ties with the National Liberal Federation. The Club was swift to live up to the incorporation of the word 'National' in its title. "Between five hundred and six hundred towns and country districts were represented among its membership".[90] Meanwhile the Reform Club could lay no such claim on its own behalf, constituencies continuing to react strongly to 'interference' in their affairs by an institution largely perceived as exclusive as well as metropolitan and unrepresentative.

---

87 Robert Steven, The National Liberal Club – Politics And Persons (London, 1920), pp.11, 14 and 15.

88 Christopher Harvie, The Lights of Liberalism: University Liberals and the Challenge of Democracy 1860-86 (London, 1976), p.128. The Radical Club, a dining club in which Sir Charles Dilke was a leading light, was founded in 1870 to combine "thinkers and writers with practising politicians". Like Dilke, J S Mill used it as a platform for his advanced views on land tenure. The Club survived until the Liberal whips effectively stifled it in 1893 by 'packing' the annual meeting at which its executive committee was elected.

89 Ostrogorski, Democracy, pp.422/423.

90 Steven, National Liberal Club, p.14, National Liberal Club, GC Minutes, 20 June 1883.

3   THE ACTIVE PHASE

'Interference' in Constituencies

Between 1870 and 1885 the minutes of the Political Committee of the Reform Club refer to over thirty constituencies by name together with an unspecified number of requests from others which are not named. The latter were usually pleas for funds. References to some of the named constituencies also included requests for assistance with election expenses, these being passed on immediately to the Liberal Central Association. Others are for speakers to address meetings and these were usually accepted for action by members of the Committee. References to the remaining named constituencies are of two sorts. They concern the conduct of members of the Club in voting for, or otherwise helping a Conservative candidate, or they involve attempts by the Political Committee to arbitrate between Liberal candidates standing for the same seat. Arbitration was usually attempted in cases of sectionalist candidates competing with a sitting mainstream Liberal member. However, disagreement could sometimes include a personal dimension, and one such case occurred immediately prior to the Political Committee's formation.

During the general election campaign of 1868 the Whiggish Lord Enfield and independent Radical, Henry Labouchere, were opposed by the youthful Lord George Hamilton in the large and electorally important constituency of Middlesex. Ostensibly this was a constituency with two 'safe' Liberal/Radical seats which the Conservatives had represented just once in the past hundred years and not at all since 1847. Following a difference of opinion, apparently over the selection of electioneering agents, Labouchere wrote to a member of the Reform Club requesting its Committee's help "in resolving the quarrel in order that one or two seats should not be lost to the Party". By this time both Enfield and Labouchere had given their respective sides of the affair at public meetings, which had received extensive coverage in the newspapers. As a result of intervention by the General Committee, Labouchere agreed to a memorandum, drafted by the Committee for the 'daily papers', in which he acknowledged the role of the Reform Club in patching up the dispute. He stated he was prepared to accept the Committee of the Reform Club's assurance that Enfield had not intended to throw doubt on his (Labouchere's) integrity. He added that he accepted also the Committee's opinion "that it is due to Lord Enfield that I should withdraw certain offensive expressions which I used concerning him and that I should now express my regret for having used them. . . I have no hesitation at once in acting on the advice of the Committee".[91] The quarrel had been satisfactorily resolved and this particular episode would seem to accord with Fraser Rae's description of the conciliatory role of the Club. Other cases were perhaps not so clear cut.

The first dispute in which the Political Committee itself played an active part concerned by-elections in the 'notoriously corrupt' borough of Norwich. On 5 July 1870 the attention of the Committee was drawn by one of its own members to two Liberal candidates contesting one seat at a forthcoming by-election. Without further ado the Committee instructed its sub-committee to "promote the success of a Liberal Candidate by healing Divisions within the Liberal Ranks". On 2 August the minutes record the satisfaction of members at the outcome including a victory at the by-election. On 2 May of the following year they record further success in reconciling divisions after yet another by-election win there.[92] No indication of the nature of the Committee's efforts is provided in the minutes, but the circumstances reported in newspapers provide more detail and a different slant on the affair. On 2 July The Times reported that a Mr Edward Warner had announced he would not contest the constituency provided a candidate who could unite the Party would come forward. However, he considered that the existing candidate Jacob Tillett, (an 'Advanced Liberal' in favour of reform of the land laws who had working class support), represented only a section of the Party and he intended to stand against him. It is worth recording at this point that Tillett had worked hard to unseat the Conservative incumbent on petition, having been unseated himself previously also on petition, and was perhaps justifiably annoyed at Warner trying to 'muscle in' on the seat at this late stage. Tillett also seems to have had the support of the bulk of local Liberals, a huge demonstration in his favour being organised on 7 July in Norwich, and a total of three thousand pledged votes recorded for him.[93] He was also supported by the local wealthy patron of the borough, J J Colman, the head of the mustard and starch firm based in Norwich. This latter factor may be the key to the Political Committee's line, for on 5 July Henry Brand, by that time its Chairman, wrote personally to Warner calling on him to "withdraw from the contest in the name of the Political Committee of the Reform Club following a resolution of that Committee". He added that if Warner did so "public opinion will confirm the view of the Committee that you are anxious. . . to do all in your power to promote the interests of the

---

91 *Reform Club, GC Minutes, 16 November 1868. Labouchere lost his seat. Hamilton won the poll. Enfield took the second seat. But the row may have had little effect on the result. Lord George wrote later: "Rapid extension of suburban railroads and the outpouring of professional men, tradesmen, and clerical employees into the rural outskirts of London had steadily changed the tone and politics of the constituency". Right Hon. Lord George Hamilton, Parliamentary Reminiscences and Reflections 1868-1906 (2 vols., London, 1922), Vol 1, p.11.*

92 *Reform Club, PC Minute Book 1, pp.65, 67 and 75.*

93 *Eastern Express, 9 July 1870.*

Liberal Party". This letter was released to The Times by Brand himself, the newspaper happily publishing it on 9 July accompanied by a reply from Warner. In his letter, an angry Warner directed his fire at the Political Committee, claiming that its attitude had had nothing to do with his decision to stand down. Furthermore, he went on to add that his knowledge of the constituency satisfies me that there is nothing they would so much resent in the conduct of a candidate as submission to the dictate of any persons whatever outside their city".[94]

It is worth noting as a postscript, in the light of the self congratulatory tone of the Political Committee's second minute recorded on 2 May 1871, that following this by-election Tillett was again unseated on petition. At yet another by-election held on 22 February 1871, Colman stood himself, apparently with some reluctance but supported by Tillett, was elected and subsequently held the seat safely for Gladstone until he retired in 1895. Neither Tillett nor Warner were members of the Reform Club, but Colman was actually elected to the Club later in 1871, his proposer being Charles de la Pryme, at the time Honorary Secretary of the Political Committee. It seems reasonable to assume that the Committee played some part in persuading him to stand himself to avoid further division, for Colman was a most respected Nonconformist of the highest integrity. "Strong pressure was put upon him. It was urged his candidature would unite both sections of the Liberal Party".[95] The role of the Political Committee in the case of Norwich does not quite accord with Fraser Rae's description, while the publicity surrounding the exchange of letters with Warner could well have been distasteful to some members of the Club.

A rather less satisfactory outcome for the Political Committee and one which drew more unfavourable publicity, stemmed from the actions of some of its members during the Aberdeen by-election of June 1872. Sir John Clark, the Liberal nominated for the seat, was forced to resign his candidature owing to ill health. James Barclay, a well known local merchant and Advanced Liberal who had originally competed unsuccessfully with Clark for the nomination, again threw his hat into the ring. He was opposed by a London barrister born in Aberdeen, John Farley Leith, an independent Liberal who called himself a Progressive Reformer, and who was also Sir John Clark's choice. Initially Leith considered it unwise to divide the Liberal vote by standing against Barclay, as a Conservative was also fighting the seat. Apparently he changed his mind following a written requisition signed by

---

94 *The Times*, 2 July 1870, p.12d and 9 July 1870, p.11b.

95 Helen Colman, *Jeremiah James Colman A Memoir* (London, 1905), pp.228-232. See also Hanham, *Elections and Party Management*, p.265 and D A Hamer, *Liberal Politics In the Age of Gladstone And Rosebery: a Study In Leadership And Policy* (Oxford, 1972), p.7.

upwards of three thousand voters. On 28 June Leith was elected, Barclay came second and the Conservative a poor third. Nevertheless at the close of the poll, Leith is reported to have addressed the electors claiming that a telegram had been received from the Political Committee of the Reform Club on 26 June saying that his Election Committee would incur a grave responsibility if he contested the seat. He went on to maintain that had he not done so the Conservative would probably have won the election and he had informed the Reform Club that the constituency of Aberdeen "would brook no interference in their selection of a Liberal candidate from any Political Club in London or elsewhere (loud applause)".[96]

References within the minutes to the Aberdeen by-election are brief. However the Political Committee's actions could be said to have laid it open to a charge of being more than just a touch 'economical with the truth'! For on 2 July an apparently authorised statement was released which read as follows:

> "The Political Committee did not take or authorise any action whatever in regard to the Aberdeen election, nor did the Club Secretary as has been alleged, send any telegrams to Aberdeen".[97]

Either second thoughts had prevailed by the following day, or members not present at the meeting on 2 July had decided to take matters into their own hands. On 4 July the following letter, to which there is no direct reference in the Political Committee's minutes, appeared in <u>The Times</u>:

> "As one of the Political Committee...I ask to be allowed to state what really did occur. In consequence of an urgent telegram received from Aberdeen. . . it was thought by some members of that Committee that some effort should be made to prevent a decision which it was then feared might be fatal to the success of the Liberal Party there.
> There was no opportunity of summoning a regular meeting but four or five members. . . determined to send to the Chairman of each Liberal Committee at Aberdeen a telegram of which the following is a copy:
>> "This Committee dreading the effect of a division in the Liberal Party, would urge in the strongest strongest manner that the Liberal candidates should should seriously examine their relative positions in order that the whole strength of the Party may be concentrated on one candidate previous to the nomination."
>
> The wording of the telegram shows that there was not the faintest attempt to dictate, or even to suggest which should be the candidate and that especial care was taken to inform each Committee that an identical message was sent to the other. . . "

---

96 <u>The Times,</u> 29 June 1872, p.9f. *The Conservative, James Shaw, actually stood as a Liberal-Conservative which tends to support Leith's contention.*

97 *Reform Club, PC Minute Book 1, p.93.*

The letter was signed 'A Member of the Political Committee of the Reform Club'.[98]

A Special Meeting was called on 30 July at which George Glyn, in an apparent reference to the offending telegram, stated that "he had acted in concert with others, under the supposition that they were doing so as a properly constituted sub-committee of the Political Committee under the Club's bye-laws. He had failed to realise that the annual delegation of such powers had not yet been authorised. The minutes record the acceptance by members of his explanation and a resolution that the subject should now be allowed to drop.[99] The views of Club members, and those of the General Committee, on the contradiction inherent in the two public statements are not recorded. Barclay was elected for Forfarshire later in the year becoming a member of the Political Committee of the Reform Club in 1879.

A growing sensitivity about the whole subject of 'arbitration' was evident in the case of the constituency of Bath, which had become one of several battlegrounds between Liberal candidates at a series of by-elections. On 22 June 1873, before one such by-election, the Political Committee passed a resolution strongly deprecating division in the Liberal ranks at Bath "as would endanger the success of a Liberal candidate". An amendment proposing substitution of the name of the officially sponsored candidate, Captain William Hayter, for the words 'a Liberal candidate' was roundly defeated by eight votes to four.[100] Hayter was a member of the Reform Club. His Liberal opponent, Mr J C Cox, sponsored by the National Education League, was not a member. Clearly some individuals on the Political Committee continued to remain insensitive to accusations of interference and partisanship, but the instinct of the majority by this time was to avoid any such accusation.[101]

It is perhaps worth including one further example of 'arbitration', this time of a rather different order. There had been a twelve year history of Liberal division at Northampton associated with the defiant free thinker and republican Radical, Charles Bradlaugh, who had so divided the Liberals in the constituency as to allow the election of two Conservatives. The local Liberal Association finally concluded that the only way to get the

---

98 *The Times*, 4 July 1872, p10b.

99 Reform Club, PC Minute Book 1, p.94.

100 Reform Club, PC Minute Book 1, p.99.

101 Hamer, *Politics of Electoral Pressure*, pp.56 and 131-133. Cox, standing as a Radical, withdrew his candidature, although he still received 13 votes at the poll on 28 June 1873. Hayter lost in any case by 51 votes to the Conservative, Viscount Grey de Wilton, in a poll of over four thousand. Hayter went on to secure the second Bath seat at another by-election in October, retaining it at the general election of 1874.

Conservatives out was to leave one of the seats to Bradlaugh.[102] Having at last been elected, Bradlaugh refused to take the oath at the bar of the House of Commons. The Speaker, Henry Brand, instead of allowing him to affirm allegiance, referred the matter to the House which voted to debar him from taking either oath or affirmation. This action triggered a series of by-elections at Northampton each of which Bradlaugh won, only to return to the House to be faced with a renewed vote for his rejection. On 21 March 1882, following one of these by-elections, a written complaint from Bradlaugh was received by the Political Committee. This alleged that one of its members, Samuel Morley MP, had written to an elector of Northampton advising him to vote for the Conservative. Bradlaugh had particular reason to feel incensed as the letter had been published by his opponent in the form of an electoral placard. The complaint put the Committee in a difficult position. No orthodox Liberal could be seen actively to support a notorious atheist in opposition to the philanthropic, pious and highly respected Morley, particularly as the latter was a member of the Political Committee. Yet a Committee which saw itself as a 'Guardian of the Spirit of Liberalism' may well have had serious misgivings about a verdict in a House of Commons with a Liberal majority which posterity might judge had been reached in a spirit of intolerance and lack of respect for the freedom of the individual. Edward Leatham proposed Bradlaugh should be informed that, as he was not a member of the Club, the Committee did not feel "at liberty to enter into the question". This somewhat disingenuous move was narrowly defeated by nine votes to eight with four abstentions, and the matter postponed for resolution at the next meeting. During the next week a consensus must have been reached 'out of Committee'. For at a Special Meeting on 28 March it was resolved, without a recorded discussion, that Bradlaugh should be informed "that in all the circumstances of the case the Committee do not propose to take any action in the matter of his complaint".[103] There the matter rested, aside from a rather bad tempered acknowledgement from Bradlaugh. However, the Northampton affair was merely one of several in which the conduct of members of the Club in providing support for Conservatives was drawn to the Political Committee's attention. Morley's action was a product of exceptional circumstances and could - just - be ignored. In the case of other

102 Trevor Lloyd, The General Election of 1880 (Oxford, 1968), p.69.

103 Reform Club, PC Minute Book 2, pp.66, 67 and 70. Sixteen of the twenty-one members attended both meetings, the only apparently significant difference being that the two whips, Lord Richard Grosvenor and Lord Kensington, were not present at the second meeting on 28 March.

offenders the Political Committee seems to have had little hesitation in initiating the process of expulsion from the Club.[104]

Expulsions on Political Grounds

In spite of periodic amendments to the Club's rules, those concerned with the expulsion of members (Rules 27, 28 and 29 in 1870) continued to require a requisition (or petition) signed by a minimum of fifty members to initiate the process. A charge of "not being a Reformer" was one of the offences specifically covered by those Rules. Having received such a requisition, the onus lay on the General Committee to communicate with the member concerned and proceed to a vote in committee as to the satisfactory nature, or not, of his reply. The first such case occurred as early as 1838 when two members were accused of voting Tory. Those attending the Special Meeting of the Committee to consider the case not only failed to make up the necessary quorum of eighteen members (it was subsequently reduced to eight) but decided anyway that it would not be "expedient" to expel the members concerned.[105] The next recorded case did not occur until 1852 and concerned a 'forced withdrawal' of a candidate for election rather than an actual expulsion. A Mr E W Cox agreed to withdraw his name from the candidates' list having been informed by the General Committee that his political opinions were not considered to be "in entire accordance with the requirements of the Club".[106] The case of Cox is clearly documented but the reasons behind nearly all 'withdrawals of candidature', as with those of blackballing, are largely a matter of speculation. For example, the Club's historian, George Woodbridge, found little evidence of any particular pattern of significance in the case of those 'not elected or withdrawn' in a general analysis covering the years between 1875 and 1932.[107] With few exceptions, Cox is one, it is impossible to be certain of political bias in individual cases. On the other hand evidence clearly exists in cases of expulsion or 'forced resignations' on ostensibly political grounds.

In July 1865 Alfred Smee, a member of the Reform, stood as a Conservative against two Liberals, also members of the Club, for the constituency of Rochester. In a pamphlet published the previous November he described Liberal supporters there as the "odds and ends of society." He abused leading Liberal families, including that of the Mayor, and also insulted his opponents by calling one of them a "dummy" and going on to describe both as no more than nominees of the Reform Club. At first, the General

---

104 The precise form of words used by Morley was apparently as follows: ". . . If I was an elector of Northampton, I should vote for the Conservative candidate. I should do this as an act of allegiance to God and to public morality, and without the slightest compromise of my attachment – never so strong as at the present moment – to Liberal principles." Edwin Hodder, The Life of Samuel Morley (New York, 1888), p.417.

105 Reform Club, GC Minutes, 24 February 1838.

106 Reform Club, GC Minutes, 20 February 1852.

107 George Woodbridge, The Reform Club 1836-1978 A history from the Club's records (Clearwater and Toronto, 1978), pp.83-89.

Committee asked him for an explanation, subsequently suggesting to him that "resignation would be conducive to the social harmony of the Club". Smee defended himself vigorously, falling back ultimately on the argument prevalent among Reformers at the time that there was little to choose between the two main political parties. For their part, the Committee was to write to him again: "the Liberal and Conservative parties are . . . sufficiently distinguished by the sides they take in the House of Commons. You propose to sit with the Conservatives. In so plain a matter, it would be useless to enter into any controversy. . ." At this point sixty-four members of the Club signed a requisition calling for a Special General Meeting in order that Smee's credentials as a genuine Reformer might be established. His resignation followed, the culmination of a process which amounted effectively to expulsion on political grounds but which may well have owed as much to Smee's 'unclubbable' language and conduct.[108]

'Unclubbability', or boorishness, was undoubtedly as large a factor in 'political expulsions' as politics itself. Following complaints that a Major Curteis had voted for the Conservative candidate at Rye, the General Committee faced a requisition signed by fifty-two members. At a Special Meeting on 25 May 1866 the Committee considered evidence in Curteis's defence. This included letters from a Trustee of the Club, the Earl of Dalhousie, and from J G Dodson MP, who was to serve in Gladstone's Second Cabinet from 1880 until he resigned in 1884. The letters testified to Curteis's Liberal principles, his qualifications as a Reformer, and of his "rendering great service to several Liberal candidates at the last election". In the event the Committee found insufficient evidence to merit expulsion concluding that Curteis's action was based on "personal objections" to the Liberal candidate, a Mr William Mackinnon, who was not a member of the Club.[109] As a postscript it is worth noting that a booklet exposing electoral corruption at Rye, and the part played in it by Mackinnon who had been unseated subsequently on petition, had been published by Major Curteis some thirteen years before this incident.[110]

These cases took place before the formation of the Political Committee, although that of Curteis was referred to in its early minutes, seemingly as part of a study of the procedures required for the expulsion of a member on political grounds. There was some early indecisiveness as to whether the Political Committee should or should not play an active role. Having drawn the attention of the General Committee to reports of antagonism to Reform during a by-election on the part of Mr W Derry, a Plymouth merchant and member of the Club for some ten years, the Political Committee accepted

---

108 *Chatham News And North Kent Spectator*. 12 and 15 *July 1865, Reform Club, GC Minutes*, 11 *November*, 2 and 23 *December 1864*, 6 *January*, 10 and 17 *February 1865*.

109 *Reform Club, GC Minutes*, 14 and 21 *July 1865*, 11 and 25 *May 1866*.

110 Major Curteis An Elector, *Exposure of the Corrupt System of Elections at Rye* (London, 1853).

that the Club's 28th Rule provided sufficient means by which Derry's conduct could be investigated should members so desire. It merely recorded its deprecation of his comments. The minutes show that the Committee then divided over a resolution that it would be inexpedient for it <u>ever</u> to interfere in such cases. Seventeen members were present. Six voted in favour of the resolution and eight against, indicating three abstentions and a clear division of opinion.[111]

At a time of waning Liberal morale as a whole, and obviously reluctant to leave the matter there, the more activist members returned to the subject of the Committee's role in cases of members whose political loyalty had been called into question. As part of an extended debate into ways in which the rules of the Club might be altered to promote its "consistent and efficient action," Edward Jenkins, supported by John Locke, put forward two proposals on 15 April 1872. These were designed to form the basis of resolutions to be put to the Annual General Meeting the next month for an increase in the powers of the Political Committee. Although their details are not recorded in the minute book, it is clear that the proposals were concerned with amendments to the Club's 28th Rule. On 15 April both were carried unanimously by the Political Committee, but second thoughts must have prevailed for fourteen days later a Special Meeting was called to re-examine the expediency of proceeding with them. At this second meeting, the Committee concluded by eight votes to three with three abstentions that the proposals should be dropped on the grounds of "the present difference of opinion on the subject".[112] It seems reasonable to assume that both proposals had sought to delegate the General Committee's authority to make the final decision on whether or not an individual member should be censured or expelled for 'defaulting' on his identity as a Reformer, to the Political Committee. It is interesting to note that the names of those members attending the meeting on 29 April had changed markedly from those who had met to vote on Jenkins's proposals on the 15th of that month. Such moderates as Richard Baxter, that 'ideal committee man', W H F Cogan, William Cowper-Temple, the Irish Liberals, Sir Patrick O Brien and N D Murphy, and Sir Alexander Brown, the last named elected to the Committee in 1871, attended the second meeting. Jenkins, Locke and perhaps Charles Robarts, who had seconded Locke's motion, were probably the three votes against withdrawal of the proposals.[113] In fact Robarts returned to the attack at a subsequent meeting proposing that the Political Committee procure a special meeting of the Club to discuss amendment of its powers. He was

111 *In the case of Derry a requisition signed by fifty-two members was eventually received by the General Committee and thrown out on the grounds that it had not specifically called for his expulsion and therefore did not conform to the letter of the Rules.*

112 *Reform Club, PC Minute Book 1, pp.88, 89 and 90.*

113 <u>Charles H Robarts</u>. *Fellow of All Souls Oxford. A Radical and one of the few 'Academic Liberals' to be elected to the Political Committee (1871), most of whom seem to have found politics too expensive. Robarts stood unsuccessfully for mid Surrey in 1868.*

firmly voted down again, this time by six votes to two with two abstentions.[114]

Despite the Political Committee's recognition that it should not attempt to be the ultimate authority in cases of censure or expulsion on political grounds, its more activist members were clearly determined that the Committee should play a major role by taking the lead in the referral of such cases to the General Committee. On 1 April 1873, the declaration of William Gordon, Tory candidate for Chelsea, was referred to the General Committee. That Committee's response is interesting in that it placed on record the method by which the 'reforming' credentials of candidates were established. Apparently neither proposer nor seconder of Gordon's nomination had included a certificate that he was a Reformer in their letters of introduction. The General Committee was swift to add an assurance that no candidate would ever be accepted for ballot without such a formal certificate under present procedures, but this was not accepted uncritically by Edward Jenkins. He sought to raise the subject at the Club's Annual General Meeting on 1 May only to be ruled out of order by the Chairman.[115] By 1874 Gordon was no longer a member of the Club.

Between 1876 and 1882 the Political Committee initiated procedures for the expulsion of at least six members on political grounds. Its actions in so doing may well have contributed to the groundswell of hostility towards the power of its committees on the part of the Club's membership, whatever the feelings on the individual personalities concerned. Indeed they may have contributed to the reasons behind the resolution at the Annual General meeting of 1885 seeking the Political Committee's own disbandment. But expulsions on such grounds after 1885 would hardly have been appropriate in any case, following the Split in the Liberal Party over Home Rule and the decision to retain Liberal Unionists as members. By 1895 three of the Club's Trustees, the Duke of Devonshire, Marquis of Lansdowne and Lord James of Hereford, were members of Lord Salisbury's Third Cabinet, the last named also the elected co-Vice-Chairman of the Political Committee at the time. However there seems little doubt from an analysis of the six cases that, as in the case of Alfred Smee, the personality of those involved played a major part in a decision to expel.

For example, the cases of Sir George Bowyer and Henry Ripley, expelled on 23 June 1876 following requisitions organised by the Political Committee and signed by one hundred and forty and one hundred and twenty-seven members respectively, suggest that personal animosity was probably a significant factor in their expulsions. These two cases generated a great deal of unfavourable publicity and could be said to have made the Club look a little foolish which can not have pleased the membership at large. Both men were expelled for not being Reformers following two votes within the General

---

114 *Reform Club PC Minute Book 1, p.91.*

115 *Reform Club, PC Minute Book 1, p.96, GC Minutes, 4 and 9 April 1873, AGM Minutes, 1 May 1873. Gordon was elected at the general election of 1874 displacing a sitting Liberal candidate, Sir Henry Hoare.*

Committee. The first recorded seven in favour of expulsion, two against and five abstentions but it was then pointed out that abstentions could not be accepted under the rules. A second vote was taken and this time ten voted in favour, three against, and one appears to have ducked the issue by leaving the room at the time the vote was taken![116] Voting against the Liberal interest, coupled with obstructive tactics in the House of Commons in conjunction with other Irish Home Rulers, was ostensibly the cause of Bowyer's 'downfall'. For example, he was one of two so-called Opposition members who helped to give the new Conservative government a majority of just three in defeating Samuel Plimsoll's Merchant Shipping Survey Bill in July 1874, conduct which enraged Liberal opinion. Bowyer was reported to have claimed he did not regret expulsion from a Club which "has systematically and persistently black-beaned every Home Rule candidate", something for which there seems to be no real evidence.[117] Admittedly there was very real anger among Liberals at the time directed at the tactics of some Irish Home Rule members who had voted with the Conservative government. Even so, in the particular case of Bowyer, personal circumstances must have played a part in what was a most controversial political career. An extract from his obituary may serve to confirm his 'unclubbability'. It refers to his ". . . unpractical obstinacy in details, and a temper which made it impossible for coadjutors to rely on his taking any particular course. . ."[118]

Henry Ripley, head of a large manufacturing firm and President of Bradford's Chamber of Commerce from 1872 to 1880, had made enemies among Nonconformists. He played a major part in keeping the leading Liberationist, Edward Miall, out of one of the parliamentary seats in the city at the general election of 1868 with the help of Conservative votes. Having been unseated on petition by Miall's supporters, his own supporters then went on to infuriate Radicals and mainstream Liberals alike by petitioning in revenge against the other successful candidate for the constituency, no less a leading Liberal than W E Forster. Forster was to enter the Cabinet the following year and could have been forgiven for feeling some personal resentment against Ripley having been the latter's proposer for membership of the Reform Club in 1864. Ripley's intemperate language, which he expressed through correspondence in <u>The Times,</u> also provides a clue to his 'unclubbability'. In one letter he maintained that the only political accountability he recognised was to the electors of Bradford, and that when he had been elected to the Reform Club "<u>no</u> conditions of political slavery

116 *Reform Club, PC Minute Book 1, pp.135/6, GC Minutes, 22 June 1876.*

117 *<u>The Times</u>, 31 July 1876, p.9f. Bowyer, Home Rule MP for Wexford, was a forceful protagonist for an Irish Parliament, but had been a member of the Reform Club since 1850.*

118 *<u>The Times</u>, 8 June 1883, p.10e. Bowyer's aggressive defence of the Papacy, following his conversion to Rome in 1850, is unlikely to have made him many friends. The failure of the Ruby Consolidated Mining Company under his chairmanship, apparently at no financial loss to himself, hardly endeared him to investors. Later his creation of an impression in Rome that the Irish Land Leaguers were "enemies of religion, the foes of morality" angered many of his fellow Home Rulers.*

were sought to be imposed upon me and I do not now require the advice of any Political Committee to guide me . . ."[119] In reading the Club's equally public riposte published on the following day and signed 'A Member of the Committee', it is relevant to bear in mind that Ripley had been elected in 1874 standing as a Liberal-Conservative:

"Sir, The question is not on what terms Mr Ripley was elected for Bradford but on what terms he was elected to the Reform Club. . . its fundamental principle is of a Society of Liberals - using that word in a party sense - and before Mr Ripley was elected his proposer and seconder had to give written assurances that he was so qualified for admission. . . Ripley has for three sessions habitually voted against the Liberal Party on party divisions, in the House of Commons, and has not had spontaneously the sense of propriety to retire from the Club.
What the Committee has done is courteously to suggest that he should retire from a Party club when he opposes its Party."[120]

On 14 June The Times, while accepting the rights of a private club as to membership, commented mockingly on what it perceived to be the Reform's lack of commonsense in contributing to a public debate over the Ripley affair:

". . . A gentleman should bow to the decree of the responsible rulers of a Club. However the Reform Club has made itself ridiculous by calling Ripley to account for his parliamentary votes and by parading to the world that it has "a Political Committee" with a special secretary attached. If the Reform Club were wise in its generation it would emulate the policy of the Committee of Brook's (sic). The late Lord Derby was a member of Brooks till (sic) the end of his life. It is comparatively quite recently that Mr Gladstone removed his name from the Carlton."[121]

Ripley lost his seat to a Liberal at the general election of 1880.

The year of 1880 proved to be a watershed for expulsions, a reflection of an unprecedented level of electioneering. The expulsion of General John de Havilland is another which might well have owed as much to personality and 'attitude' as to domestic party politics. A requisition, signed by fifty-four members and organised by the Political Committee, called for his expulsion on the grounds that he was not a Reformer having ". . . driven to the poll in a carriage displaying the Tory colours and himself wore evidence of such partisanship". The minute books are full of the acrimonious correspondence between the Committee and an outspoken General, including one reply from de Havilland in which he claimed that to have asked him to disclose his

---

119 The Times, 3 June 1876, p.8c, Reform Club, PC Minute Book 1, p.135.

120 The Times, 3 June 1876, p.9c.

121 The Times, 14 June 1876, p.14c. See also text related to note 34.

voting intentions was illegal under the Ballot Act.[122] He went on to add that half the Reform Club's members, if polled, would vote for the Conservatives. However, some four years previously there had been speculation within the Political Committee that the General was not really entitled to be addressed as such, his rank having been conferred on him in the service of Don Carlos of Spain rather than by a duly constituted government.[123] It seems that de Havilland had been Secretary of the Carlist Committee in London, a Movement which refused to recognise the legitimacy of the current Spanish royal house. Liberal sensitivities on this subject were high. The famous soldier and one time Radical MP, Colonel de Lacy Evans, had commanded the British Legion which fought for the Spanish Constitutionalists against the Carlists in the 1830s. During the campaign a number of prisoners among the legionaries were summarily executed by the Carlists. Ultimately de Havilland was expelled on 18 June 1880, the vote within the General committee being seven in favour, two against expulsion, one apparent abstention and one member who left the room'. [124]

The expulsion of the Irish Nationalist member for Dundalk, Philip Callan, provides further support for the possibility that personal dislike in the face of unclubbable conduct played no small part in 'bringing to the boil' cases of members arraigned on the grounds of 'political deviation'. A first attempt to expel Callan was made in 1880. It failed on the rather curious grounds of his pleading ill health as an excuse for his 'conduct', suggesting perhaps some ill considered words or deed while not totally in command of his faculties! David Thornley specifically names Callan as a member of the Reform Club expelled for voting against the Liberal Party and, two years later, a second attempt to expel him did succeed at a time of strong feelings among MPs following the murders in Phoenix Park Dublin.[125] However, like de Havilland, Callan supported the Carlist cause and in any case seems to have offended most of those with whom he came into political contact.[126] An original follower of Charles Stewart Parnell in 1877 and suspended with him from the House of Commons for obstruction on 1 July 1882, Callan was cordially disliked by his leader who effectively drove him out of politics in 1885. Callan can hardly have been exactly popular with Gladstonian Liberals either having

---

122 *Reform Club, PC Minute Book 2, pp.38-40 and 43-45, GC Minutes, 9 and 23 April and 4, 11 and 18 June 1880.*

123 *Reform Club, PC Minute Book 1, p.128.*

124 *PC Minute Book 2, pp.38-40 and 43-45, GC Minutes, 9 and 23 April and 4, 11 and 18 June 1880.*

125 *Reform Club, PC Minute Book 2, pp.36 and 42, GC Minutes, 22 and 29 October 1880, 4 November 1880 and 12 May 1882, D A Thornley, <u>Isaac Butt and The Home Rule Party</u> (London, 1964), p.217. The murders of Lord Frederick Cavendish, the newly appointed Chief Secretary for Ireland, and T H Burke, a senior civil servant at Dublin Castle, on 6 May. A member of the Club wrote of the outrage: "...Reform Club was besieged with inquiries...[it was] naturally supposed that authentic news would be procurable at the 'Ministerialist' Club." See Stuart J Reid (ed.), <u>Memoirs of Sir Wemyss Reid 1842-1885</u> (London, 1905), p.324.*

126 <u>*Wexford People,*</u> *28 February 1874.*

displaced Chichester Fortescue from his family seat in Louth in 1874 which the latter had held for the Liberals since 1847. On a more personal note Fortescue had also been one of Callan's proposers for membership of the Reform Club in 1869, which may have weighed heavily with members. Callan proceeded to add further insult to injury by electing to sit for Dundalk, rather than Louth, where his candidature had also been successful.

Attempts to expel two other members in 1880, Charles Liddell and William Brownrigg Elliot, do seem to have been based on clear cut political grounds. This is borne out by later efforts of members to restore Liddell's membership and the failure of the requisition against Elliot. Both men were accused of supporting Conservative candidates. Liddell, a member of the Club for over twenty-five years, was reported to have spoken on a public platform in favour of the sitting (Conservative) MP for Rye, John Gathorne Hardy, who had just completed a speech in favour of Disraeli's foreign policy and against Home Rule. Commenting that since Hardy first came forward in the constituency "he had thought it right to oppose the policy of Mr Gladstone (applause)", Liddell added that having "been with the Liberal Party all his life and a member of the Reform Club for thirty years", he would continue to support Hardy in the future.[127] Having made such a public statement in a marginal constituency, Liddell's subsequent attempt to explain himself was dismissed as unsatisfactory by the General Committee and he was expelled from the Club on 4 June 1880. It is interesting to note that Hardy's successful opponent at Rye in that general election (by just eight votes) was Frederick Inderwick, a highly respected member of the Reform Club. Inderwick was elected to the Political Committee some two weeks before Liddell's expulsion was ordered. He was also a member of the General Committee for twenty-three years and Chairman for eight of those years. Liddell's membership was never restored to him.

Elliot, on the other hand, a member of the staunchly Whiggish Minto family, escaped expulsion. He was reported to have written to Sir George Douglas, the Conservative opponent at Roxburghe of his kinsman, Arthur Elliot, expressing his amazement that the latter had found it impossible to condemn Gladstone's 'unstatesmanlike' campaign against Disraeli's foreign policy. In the same letter he also condemned the Liberal Party for playing "fast and loose with the existence of the Established Church of Scotland and for having truck with Home Rule". Finally he went on to refer to the "cowardly treatment" Douglas had received from Liberal supporters at a recent meeting at Kelso and made it clear he would vote for Douglas at the forthcoming election.[128] The letter was all the more remarkable because the two rival houses of Douglas and Elliot had waged a political struggle to represent the marginal seat of Roxburghe since the 17th Century. Arthur

127 *South Eastern Advertiser*, 20 March 1880.

128 *Kelso Mail*, 31 March 1880.

Elliot, who won the seat from Douglas by just ten votes in 1880, became a Liberal Unionist in 1886 and the two families finally became political allies. Perhaps William Brownrigg Elliot's close connection with the Earl of Minto helped his cause with the General Committee. During the same meeting at which Liddell was expelled its members, although finding his conduct opposed "to the interests of the Club", nevertheless found his explanation acceptable "having regard to all the circumstances of the case".[129] Gladstone's crusading condemnation of Disraeli's foreign policy between 1876 and 1879, even as it re-united most Liberals under one banner in 1880, contributed to a growing disenchantment among many at the higher social levels of the Party. A number of prominent Whig families, together with other lesser lights among the squirearchy and plutocracy, left the Party at this time.[130]

An Irritated Club Membership And The Chamberlain Affair

Attempts by the Political Committee to involve itself in the affairs of individual constituencies can not be described as a success. The Committee would perhaps have been better employed in concentrating upon raising funds, finding speakers for political meetings, and working through members of the Club who were influential in individual constituencies, as it appears ultimately to have done in the case of the by-elections in Norwich in late 1870 and early 1871. This point was made with some force by the writer of a leading article in the Liberal and Radical in 1887. Commenting on the collective political involvement of members of the National Liberal Club, let alone the Reform, he emphasised that Clubs were not elected representative bodies:

> "It is to the properly elected county and borough associations we look to take the political action required by their respective localities. . . For the Club to take any part in local politics and interfere with free local action would be the most suicidal policy"[131]

Nor can it be said that the Committee's leading role in attempts to expel individual members for 'political disloyalty' enhanced its reputation within as well as outside the walls of the Club. For there had already been signs as early as mid 1880 of a growing restiveness among members towards the powers of committees in relation to such expulsions, whatever the degree of personal unpopularity of an individual.

During the meeting on 18 June 1880, at which the decision to expel de Havilland was finally taken, the General Committee was also faced with a

---

129 *Reform Club, GC Minutes, 4 June 1880.*

130 *An interesting article on the changing centre of political gravity of the Liberal Party, written some ten years later, analysed Liberal defections during Gladstone's crusade against Disraeli's 'use of military power for imperial aggrandisement' which culminated in the former's 'Midlothian campaign' before the general election of 1880. See* Speaker, *11 January 1890.*

131 Liberal and Radical, *3 December 1887.*

requisition, signed by one hundred and sixty members, asking for a Special General Meeting. This demanded consideration of a modification of the rules concerned with expulsion on political grounds, so as to include the right of appeal to such a Meeting. One hundred and thirteen members subsequently attended the Special Meeting held on 8 July, only to be informed that the General Committee had already decided that the time was right for a general review of all the Club's rules. Clearly a 'piece of fancy footwork' by James Caird, the Chairman of the General Committee. At the time he was also a member of the Political Committee which he had consulted during its meeting on 6 July.[132]

Three resolutions placed before the Annual General Meeting of 1881, aimed at curtailing the power of the Club's Committees, suggest that a number of members remained dissatisfied and continued to press for substantial changes to the rules. The first proposed that no member of the Political Committee should also serve on the General Committee. The second proposed that an appeal procedure should be introduced in the case of expulsions. The third, ruled out of order by the Chairman, sought to restore Charles Liddell's membership. The first two resolutions obtained majorities in favour at the Meeting. However, procedures under the rules effectively allowed an appeal against resolutions carried at Annual General Meetings through an amending motion put down at the time seeking a separate ballot of the membership at a Special General Meeting. Both resolutions were lost at such a ballot held on 19 May, the hierarchy of the Club presumably having mobilised enough support to defeat them, although by 1882 the wishes of members had prevailed. The rules were changed to allow a final decision in cases of expulsion on the grounds of not being a Reformer to be referred to a Special General Meeting of the whole membership. In this same year the 'struggle' between membership and committees spilled over into the public domain, with successful resistance on the part of members to a proposal to enhance the powers of the General Committee in relation to the election of candidates. This followed a case of blackballing, which aroused considerable public interest, and culminated in a civil action for damages.[133]

On 9 March 1882 the two younger brothers of Joseph Chamberlain, Walter and Herbert, were blackballed by more than sixty members of the Reform Club, following a period of some two years on the candidates' waiting list. Six days later the <u>Leeds Mercury</u> carried an article seeking to counter accusations and/or innuendo which had presumably originated with the Chamberlains:

"Birmingham Liberalism would only make itself ridiculous if it were to

---

[132] Reform Club, SGM Minutes, 8 July 1880, PC Minute Book 2, pp. 49 and 50.

[133] Reform Club, Annual Report, 14 April 1881, AGM Minutes, 5 May 1881, AGM Minutes 4 May 1882.

ORIGINAL DRAWING.

THE MORNING ROOM

PRESENTED TO THE REFORM CLUB BY T

1 Sir Arthur D. Hayter, Bart.
2 Right Hon. Lord Kensington
3 Right Hon. Viscount Hampden, G.C.B
4 Right Hon. H. Campbell-Bannerman, M.P.
5 Right Hon. J.T. Hibbert
6 Sir Sydney H. Waterlow, Bart.
7 Right Hon. Earl Spencer, K.G., &c.
8 Sir Andrew Lusk, Bart.
9 The Most Noble the Marquis of Ripon, K.G.
10 Right Hon. J.B. Balfour, M.P.
11 W.S. Caine, Esq.
12 Sir Wilfrid Lawson, Bart., M.P.
13 W. Woodall, Esq., M.P.
14 Right Hon. H.H. Fowler, M.P.
15 Leonard Courtney, Esq., M.P.
16 Sir Edward W. Watkin, Bart., M.P.
17 Jacob Bright, Esq., M.P.
18 H.L.W. Lawson, Esq., M.P.
19 H.D. Pochin, Esq.
20 Joseph Cowen, Esq.

THE REFORM CLUB.

PROPRIETORS OF "ILLUSTRATED LONDON NEWS."

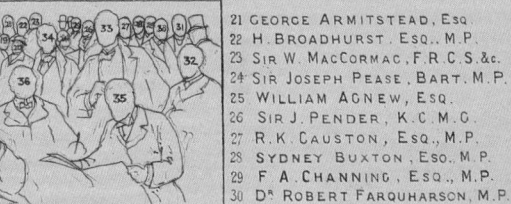

21 GEORGE ARMITSTEAD, ESQ.
22 H. BROADHURST, ESQ., M.P.
23 SIR W. MACCORMAC, F.R.C.S. &c.
24 SIR JOSEPH PEASE, BART. M.P.
25 WILLIAM AGNEW, ESQ.
26 SIR J. PENDER, K.C.M.G.
27 R. K. CAUSTON, ESQ., M.P.
28 SYDNEY BUXTON, ESQ. M.P.
29 F. A. CHANNING, ESQ., M.P.
30 Dr. ROBERT FARQUHARSON, M.P.
31 SIR C. CAMPBELL, K.C.S.I., M.P.
32 RIGHT HON. SIR H. JAMES, Q.C., M.P.
33 RIGHT HON. SIR W. C. VERNON HARCOURT, Q.C., M.P.
34 RIGHT HON. SIR G. O. TREVELYAN, BART. M.P.
35 RIGHT HON. EARL OF ROSEBERY.
36 RIGHT HON. EARL GRANVILLE, K.G.
37 THE RIGHT HON. MARQUIS OF HARTINGTON, M.P.
38 SIR CHARLES RUSSELL, Q.C., M.P.
39 RIGHT HON. A. J. MUNDELLA, M.P.
40 HERBERT J. GLADSTONE, ESQ., M.P.

raise an outcry against the members of the Reform Club for exercising a right of which nobody can deprive them. . . it is entirely untrue that there is any movement against 'Advanced Liberalism' in the club. . . That . . . is not the cause of the black-balling of the two gentlemen from Birmingham. [134]

The particular significance of the Leeds Mercury, in the context of the Reform Club, lay in the personality of its editor at the time. Thomas Wemyss Reid, editor from 1870 to 1887, had been 'taken up' by W E Baxter, an original member of the Political Committee, when the former was running the newspaper's London office and the latter Secretary of the Admiralty in Gladstone's First Administration. In his memoirs Wemyss Reid suggests that the blackballing of the Chamberlain brothers arose from the anger of moderate Liberals at Joseph Chamberlain's efforts to undermine his Cabinet colleague, W E Forster, the Chief Secretary for Ireland. Forster resigned that appointment a few weeks later.[135] Wemyss Reid was also a friend of Herbert Gladstone, who had been elected as MP for Leeds in 1880, and of Forster himself, who had been Reid's proposer for membership of the Reform Club. Feelings were running very high over Ireland in the Spring of 1882 with Forster's policy of coercion deemed to have failed by the Cabinet.[136] Following his editorship of the Leeds Mercury, Wemyss Reid went on to edit the Speaker from 1890 to 1897, and to play a major role in the Club's affairs. Elected in 1878, he became a member of the Political Committee in 1887 and Chairman of the General Committee from 1897 to 1901 and from 1903 to 1905.

The public row over the blackballing, following the membership's attempt at the Annual General Meeting in May 1881 to curtail the powers of its Committees, seems to have galvanised the Political Committee into undertaking a review of the way in which the other seven London 'political clubs' elected candidates. A review sub-committee concluded that the Reform was unique in not entrusting the process to its General Committee, which was half the size by 1882 (fifteen members) of those of other clubs. It recommended effectively that General and Political Committees should amalgamate their functions with these undertaken in future by a committee of thirty members, and that no less than the Lords Hartington and Granville should be approached to move or support such a resolution.[137] The Political

134 Leeds Mercury, 15 March 1882.

135 Stuart J Reid (ed.), Memoirs of Sir Wemyss Reid 1842-1885 (London, 1905), pp. 152 and 329.

136 In the first week of May Parnell and his three parliamentary colleagues, imprisoned without trial the previous October, were released under the terms of the notorious 'Kilmainham Treaty' between the government and Parnell, with which Chamberlain had been closely and clandestinely associated, thereby cutting the ground from under the feet of the Chief Secretary.

137 Reform Club, PC Minute Book 2, pp.71-73. The seven clubs were Carlton, Junior Carlton, City Carlton, Conservative, St Stephen's, City Liberal and Devonshire Clubs.

Committee endorsed the recommendation. Eighteen days later the General Committee considered a draft motion from Lord Hartington that in future all candidates should be elected by committee and resolved that this should be put in the form of a resolution at the Annual General Meeting on 4 May. Hartington's motion was seconded by John Bright, thus giving it ministerial support from both Whig and Radical wings of the Party. On 4 May it was finally decided that the issue should be put to a separate ballot of the membership on 18 May.[138] The minutes of the Club's Committees do not record the result of that ballot, but it was reported in the Spectator that the resolution had been lost by twenty-one votes in a total poll of seven hundred and forty-three members, apparently the heaviest vote ever recorded at the Club. The result confirms the presence of a substantial body among the membership who could be said to have concluded that the ruling Committees of the Club were already quite powerful enough and certainly should not be allowed to interfere "in the right of every true-born Englishman to black-ball anyone he pleased at a club election."[139]

The Spectator's report provides an insight into the difficulties of probing the true role of the members of a private club in public affairs, not least in the era of the Victorian gentleman. It refers to the right of newspapers on this specific occasion to disregard "etiquette which protects the recent dispute in the Reform Club from public discussion". It also places on record, two months after Wemyss Reid's denial in the Leeds Mercury of any 'campaign' against Radicals, a continuing public perception of the exclusivity of the Reform and of its domination by the Whigs. It even 'dares' to make a judgement on members' lack of support for the resolution:

> "The vote [at the ballot] was in fact the culmination of a quarrel between two 'couches sociales' which has been raging for a long time within the Liberal Party. . . The real question at issue was whether persons who have become important in politics, but who are not known to the aristocratic section of the Liberals, or not liked by them, shall be admitted into, Political Clubs. . . The Reform Club cannot hinder Mr Chamberlain's friends from becoming powerful by excluding them from its walls. . . A Committee is almost certain in such cases to see further than it electors. . ."[140]

Ironically it was the 'high priest' of Whiggism, Lord Hartington himself, who had put the resolution seeking to increase the power of the Committee and thus reduce the membership's scope for 'unreasonable' blackballing of candidates. To be fair to the Spectator, it did acknowledge Hartington's

---

138 *Reform Club, GC Minutes, 21 April 1882, AGM Minutes, 4 May 1882.*

139 *T Wemyss Reid, Life Of The Rt Hon W E Forster (New York, 1920), p.330, and quoted by Marsh, Joseph Chamberlain, p.142.*

140 *Spectator, 20 May 1882.*

authorship later in its article, but failed to draw the obvious conclusion that the thrust of its 'couche sociale' argument might therefore be wide of the mark. Hartington was reported later to have written to the Club's Chairman, James Caird, following the result of the ballot. The contents of his letter are not recorded, but apparently had the effect of pre-empting any reaction from Chamberlain's supporters. For at the next ballot on 8 June none of the fourteen candidates were blackballed, although Chamberlain resigned from the Club and went on to sue a member of the General Committee, Edward Lennox Boyd, whom he implied had been responsible for the blackballing by spreading lies about his brothers. Judgement was ultimately given for the defendant, The Times commenting in a leader that the affair's link to an attempt involving Cabinet Ministers to change the rules of the Club had amounted to a "grave party question".[141]

---

141 *The Times*, 13 December 1882, p.9b. Lennox Boyd was to be elected to the Political Committee in 1884, but allowed 'his tongue to run away with him again' just one year later and was forced to resign.

4 DIVISION AND A RETREAT FROM POLITICS

The 'Attack' On The Political Committee

The resentment of members at the power of the Club's Committees should be seen in the wider context of the record of the Liberal Party following its victory at the general election of 1880. This was a period when many divisions came to the surface, reaching a climax with the split over Home Rule for Ireland in 1886. The years between 1880 and 1885 are 'distinguished' by bad temper, frustration, opportunism and disunity within both Liberal and Conservative Parties. A Liberal Administration, unexpectedly returned to power with little positive or constructive within its manifesto, became 'bogged down' in the Bradlaugh case and largely futile attempts to avoid being "crushed between the forceps of coercion and conciliation" in its Irish policy.[142] Charles Stewart Parnell's parliamentary tactics of obstruction destroyed much of the political coherence which remained. Ministers were divided over policy. Rank and file Liberals squabbled over priorities and the lack of progress in bringing forward their chosen bills. Radicals were further split over Irish coercion and Middle Eastern policy, particularly following the resignation of John Bright from the Cabinet in July 1882. Gladstone was seventy-five by the New Year of 1885 and once again talked frequently of retirement. The Radicals were determined that if, as seemed likely, Lord Hartington succeeded him it would be on their terms. In spite of apparently successful Radical pressure leading to further extension of the franchise, and to a major redistribution of parliamentary seats, morale among Liberal MPs fell to the point where there were sixty-two MPs absent and unpaired at the government's defeat on the vote on Second Reading of the Budget on 8 June 1885. Interestingly, only one of these was among the thirty-two MPs on the Political Committee, further evidence perhaps of its majority's continuing loyalty towards Gladstone.

Trouble within the Club broke out in May 1884 in the form of a full blown row between Political and General Committees. Several ostensibly unconnected incidents were responsible. On 26 May 1884 Edward Leatham and Walter James, members of both committees, resigned in pique from the Political Committee after defeat of the former's resolution to elect John Carvell Williams to the Club under Rule IV. Leatham was a highly respected 'Independent Liberal', Vice-Chairman of the General Committee and its Chairman elect for the following year. Carvell Williams was a controversial Radical lawyer who had campaigned vigorously for many years for Disestablishment of the Church of England in association with the leading Liberationist, Edward Miall. He had been Parliamentary Secretary of the

---

142 H C G Matthew (ed.), *The Gladstone Diaries With Cabinet Minutes And Prime-Ministerial Correspondence. Volume X January 1881-June 1883*, (Oxford, 1990), p.cix.

Liberation Society since 1877, also Chairman of its Executive Committee, and had frequently organised support for sectional parliamentary candidates, sometimes at the expense of those representing mainstream Liberalism. However, by 1884, he had moderated his views and was now advocating co-operation between Party and Society, and loyalty towards Gladstone. Thus Carvell Williams should have been able to count on the support not just of long standing advocates of Disestablishment such as Leatham but of fellow Welsh Liberals in the shape of Morgan Lloyd and Lewis Morris, of prominent Dissenters such as Samuel Morley and Joseph Pease, and even of orthodox tolerant Liberalism in the shape of Andrew Lusk, all of them members of the Political Committee in 1884. Uniquely the Committee failed to reach a unanimous decision to elect him, as it was required to do under Rule IV. Urged "in earnest hope" to withdraw their resignations on the grounds that a committee's duties can not "fitly be discharged without the necessary exercise of mutual concession", both Leatham and James brusquely declined.[143] By the middle of 1884 it could reasonably be concluded that at least two members of the General Committee were thoroughly out of sympathy with its political counterpart.

The same period saw one clear cut difference of opinion and one major misunderstanding arise between the two committees. At meetings in late May and early June the Political Committee resolved to approach other London Liberal clubs with a view to forming a joint body, to include also the Liberal whips, whose task it would be to promote common political action within the "organisation of the Liberal Party in the metropolis and the immediate neighbourhood".[144] In the light of division within the Party, it is hardly surprising that this particular initiative failed to achieve a single joint meeting, let alone any 'common political action'. The Political Committee finally accepted the uselessness of proceeding with the venture in early May 1885, some five weeks before the resignation of the Liberal government following defeat on the Budget in the House of Commons, the technical cause of the government's downfall.[145] Meanwhile the General Committee made clear its displeasure with the Political Committee for not having consulted formally before approaching other clubs. This produced the somewhat brisk, perhaps even 'insubordinate' riposte that the latter, as the political focus for the Club's activities, assumed the former was referring only to permission for the use of a room at the Club if this was required for a joint meeting.[146]

At the same time a major misunderstanding led to a sharp exchange of letters on the subject of the Political Committee's reaction to a circular

---

143 Reform Club, PC Minute Book 2, pp.92, 95, 96 and 99.

144 Reform Club, PC Minute Book 2, pp.98 and 117.

145 The Devonshire and City Liberal Clubs agreed to look at the idea, but Brooks's and the new National Liberal Club refused to participate from the start.

146 Reform Club, PC Minute Book 2, p.106.

requesting the Club to send delegates to a demonstration at Hyde Park on 30 June in support of the Franchise Bill. The Bill, to become the first part of the 'Third Reform Act' (of 1884/1885) was being fiercely contested in the Lords. Meanwhile Radicals were encouraging the organisation of rallies in support of the cry of 'peers against the people', Hyde Park being an obvious and emotive venue for such events. The Park had occupied a special place as a symbol of political liberty in the face of oligarchic privilege since the Reform League's 'demonstrations' of 1866 and 1867. The Political Committee, fully aware of the controversial nature of any action it might take in support of the organisers of the demonstration, was careful to make clear in correspondence that it was not the custom of its members to represent the Club at public meetings. Unfortunately, it appears that the organisers had already implicated the Club by publishing the names of 'sympathetic' members of the Committee, including those who had been delegated to attend a preliminary meeting following receipt of the circular. On 4 July the General Committee, faced with a requisition signed by over eighty members of the Club demanding an Extraordinary General Meeting to discuss the implications of the Political Committee's 'resolution to send a deputation to Hyde Park', received a belated assurance that no such action had been authorised on behalf of the Club. However a motion, most notably seconded by Edward Lennox Boyd, a member of both General and Political Committees, placed on record the former's view that any misunderstanding which had arisen within the Club was the fault of the Political Committee in not keeping it properly informed.

On 15 July the latter replied regretting the misunderstanding, but pointed out that a political matter affecting the Club was its affair and "one with which no other Club authority has any power to interfere." The part played by Lennox Boyd, the same individual sued by Joseph Chamberlain following the blackballing of his brothers, seems to have been the cause of the 'rise in temperature' among members of the Political Committee. Claiming that his presence at the relevant meetings of both committees should have prevented any misunderstanding, the Political Committee resolved that he had misrepresented its position throughout the Club. He had been guilty of "disloyalty to his colleagues. . . as to constitute 'ungentlemanly conduct' thereby disqualifying him as a fit member of the Reform Club. . ." Only Lennox Boyd's swift acceptance of the advice of its Chairman, to resign from the Political Committee, avoided a requisition for expulsion and achieved withdrawal of the resolution. At this stage at least three of the fifteen members of the General Committee, including its Chairman elect, could be said to have looked with disfavour on their sister committee.[147]

There appears to have been little politically remarkable about Mr Francis

---

147 *Reform Club, PC Minute Book 2, pp.101 and 104-109, GC Minutes, 27 June and 4 July 1884.*

Tagart, who stood up at the Club's Annual General Meeting on 5 May 1885 and proposed the abolition of its Political Committee. He was sixty-six years old at the time, a one time London merchant and Chairman of the Surrey docks, who had fought Mid Somerset unsuccessfully for the Liberals in 1868, but does not seem to have made another attempt to enter Parliament. A member of the Reform Club since 1878, he became an active Liberal Unionist in 1886, and died in 1911 at the age of ninety-two years. The expression 'stalking horse' comes to mind in assessing his role in the affair, and there is no other reference to him in those records of the Club which are of a political nature. The Political Committee received notice of his motion, but its members do not seem to have taken it seriously agreeing to leave it to individuals to respond. At the Annual General Meeting Charles Villiers, by then eighty-three years old, moved a successful amendment to Tagart's motion. Villiers proposed that before any vote was taken the Political Committee should submit a report on its activities, which would be circulated to members before the next Annual Meeting. A counter proposal, demanding a ballot of the whole membership on Tagart's motion at a Special General Meeting was then submitted, allowed by the Chairman, and fixed for 21 May. Some days later the General Committee refused to uphold a complaint from the Political Committee that the ballot should be cancelled. The complaint was based on the technical grounds that the proposal for a ballot had not been put properly by the Chairman, and therefore not actually voted upon at the Annual General Meeting.[148] Consequently planning for the ballot went ahead.

Meanwhile the relationship between the two committees declined further with the issue of a rebuke by the General Committee over 'improper' use of the Club's stationery in the form of a circular from the Political Committee arguing its case in advance of the ballot, and addressed to all members of the Club. This particular row rumbled on until July, continuing even after the defeat of Tagart's resolution by two hundred and fifty-seven to one hundred and forty-three votes at the ballot. At one stage the Political Committee went so far as to issue formal protests over the impounding of addressed envelopes used for its circular and over the General Committee's decision to forbid the Club's Assistant Secretary from devoting any of his time to its service.[149] It is relevant to the Political Committee's case that May 1885 was hardly an appropriate time for the major party political club of the Liberal Party to be seen to be disbanding its political organisation. A general election was due within a year, while the disunity of the Party had never been more apparent at such a critical time. An exhausted and ill Prime Minister in his mid seventies, who had spent the month in open abdication of his responsibility for leadership, presided over a Cabinet more divided than ever on the way

148 Reform Club, PC Minute Book 2, p.118, AGM Minutes, 7 May 1885, GC Minutes, 21 May 1885.

149 Reform Club, PC Minute Book 2, pp.122-126 and Minute Book 3, pp.2-10, GC Minutes, 15 May, 12 June and 3 July 1885.

forward for its Irish policy. Morale within Cabinet and among backbench MPs sank to the point where the Cabinet resigned office on 9 June without any attempt to reverse defeat on the Second Reading of the Budget. Equally, for the Political Committee to devote much of its attention that same June, and in July, to bad tempered bickering over the use of the Club's stationery, was hardly to do justice either to the political situation of the Liberal Party at that time.

Little more of substance was heard from the full Committee in 1885. The sub-committee met on 12 October to agree participation on behalf of the Club in a joint committee, representing all metropolitan Liberal clubs, and deputed to appoint a list of arbitrators to settle claims for the same seat between contending Liberal candidates at the forthcoming general election. Nominations from the Devonshire Club, claimed by its Committee to have been "selected not from association with any political club but because their position in the Liberal Party was such as to command the confidence and respect of all sections", were ultimately agreed by the joint committee. These were the Marquis of Hartington, Sir Henry James, Samuel Morley, Joseph Chamberlain and John Morley, only the first three named being members of the Reform Club in 1885.[150] The Board of Arbitration met on a number of occasions and seems to have had some success, for example the withdrawal of the candidature of a Mr Partridge for the constituency of Walworth, following his reluctant acceptance of the Board's ruling.[151]

The results of the general election of November 1885 could not be hailed as a success by either of the major political parties. While newly enfranchised miners and agricultural workers were no doubt responsible for increasing Liberal representation in rural constituencies, substantial losses in the boroughs could be put down to the government's record, Anglican suspicion of Nonconformist candidates, and Irish opposition. These more than offset the gains in the counties while Parnell's Irish Home Rule Party, now increased to eighty-six members, found itself holding the balance of power. Disappointment among members of the Reform Club at the result of the general election was directed at parliamentary candidates who had refused arbitration and divided the Liberal vote. On 4 December 1885 the General Committee took the extreme action of ordering that a 'black list' of such seats should be published within the Club. The name of each candidate, annotated accordingly if a member of the Club, was placed against the constituency concerned. Resignations reached an abnormal level over this period, for example a total of sixteen recorded at the General Committee's meeting of 8 January 1886. Meanwhile, following clear signs of its unpopularity within the Club and its secondary role in the initiative to form a Board of Arbitration before the election, it is significant that the Political Committee played no

---

150 *Reform Club, PC Minute Book 3, pp.14-16.*

151 *The Times. 7 November 1885, pp.7a and 10f and 12 November 1885, p. 10a. See also Reform Club, PC Minute Book 3, pp. 12 and 22 and National Liberal Club, GC Minutes, 9 December 1885.*

part in the arrangements for preparing and posting up the Club's 'black list.' It did not meet until February and by then its members were engaged in the preparation of the Report of its activities since its formation, which the Chairman had engaged to produce for the Club's next Annual General Meeting.

Thus while Liberal and Conservative leaders, faced by a hung parliament, played "a complex game of political poker", each concerned to preserve party unity while circling "warily around the poisoned chalice of Home Rule",[152] the Political Committee of the Reform Club concerned itself with drafting a defence of its own record. It continued to do so once Gladstone had opted to form an Administration at the end of January, and firmly decided to promote Home Rule for Ireland as the 'single great unifying issue' of his Third Administration. To be fair to the Committee there was probably little it could have known, or was able to do, about the process in any case. A rejuvenated, if politically reclusive Gladstone, who had made clear that his continuing leadership would be devoted only to the issue of Ireland, hardly kept the Cabinet itself informed of the substance of the Bill until the last moment. Gladstone's motives in raising the standard of Home Rule for Ireland have been much discussed among historians. Few doubt his perception of a moral dimension to the issue. However, in the light of his government's record between 1880 and 1885, and Gladstone's own leaning towards single issue politics, Home Rule must also be seen as a colossal gamble to provide a squabbling and divided Party with just such an overriding and so obviously Liberal issue around which it could rally. His failure to 'pull off' the gamble effectively stemmed the tide of history on which Radicals had been counting. For it created an apparently new ideological division, not just within the Liberal Party, but among Radicals themselves. The high ground of British politics became that of the unity of empire and kingdom to the advantage of the Conservatives, who were to occupy it for all but three of the next twenty years.

For its part the Political Committee had completed its Report, a final draft of which was signed by Charles Villiers on 28 April, the Annual General Meeting being scheduled for 6 May. Unsurprisingly the Report was defensive in nature, perhaps in the absence of much in the way the Committee could claim, at least openly, of solid achievement. The report covered some seven general areas: a reference to those of its original members who were still alive: its terms of reference: its modus operandi including times of meetings and numbers required to make up a quorum: a list of those elected under Rule IV including a reference to the one candidate it had rejected, and emphasising its belief that this had been the cause of the motion for its abolition: a defence of

---

152 Malcolm Pearce and Geoffrey Stewart, <u>British Political History 1867-1990 Democracy and Decline</u> (London, 1992), p.90.

its actions on individual expulsions: a list of its activities over the years highlighting the 'promotion of harmony' within the Party and, surely with tongue firmly in cheek, service to organised labour making much of its 'token' election under Rule IV of "a representative of the working class, Mr Thomas Burt", to the Club. Finally it contained a comprehensive list of past officers of the Committee, and ended by welcoming suggestions for reforms of its constitution "which might benefit the Club and prove of service to the Liberal Party". Unfortunately, the actual submission of the Report did little to improve the Committee's relationship with the rest of the Club. It was handed, quite deliberately it appears, to the Secretary immediately before the start of the Annual General Meeting of 6 May 1886, thus effectively preventing much in the way of discussion of its contents. A copy of the full Report, bar its preamble, is at Appendix 3.[153]

The 'Split' Of 1886

Both contemporary and modern writers have testified to the strength of feeling over Home Rule for Ireland in 1886. Animosity was not confined to divided Liberal constituency associations and political clubs but spilled over into drawing rooms throughout the country. It reached into the intellectual and literary society of the capital, and into the universities where a dominant and cohesive Liberalism now turned Unionist. It damaged relationships between close friends and members of the same family.[154] ". . . no Unionist could have asked either H. [Sir William Harcourt] or S. [Earl Spencer] to dine without receiving the assent of their guests to meet them".[155] The Queen, in barely concealed even unconstitutional partisanship, led the social boycott of those few peers, for example the Earls Spencer and Kimberley, who supported Home Rule and remained loyal to Gladstone. Jonathan Parry emphasises the haemorrhage of 'propertied wealth' from the Liberal cause, estimating that by 1892 only some 15% of county magistrates remained Liberals.[156] Many Unionists, whether politically active or not, believed Home Rule to be a potentially mortal blow to the fundamental principle of the British Constitution. Their point of view was put forcibly by the contemporary Liberal jurist and academic, Albert Venn Dicey, brother of

---

153 Reform Club, AGM Minutes, 6 May 1886. The apparent original of the Report exists. See Reform Club mss., Box 9. A verbatim copy was also written into the Political Committee's minutes at PC Minute Book 2, pp.36-46.

154 G Shaw Lefevre, 'The Liberal Split', Nineteenth Century, XX (1886), pp.597/8, G M Trevelyan, Sir George Otto Trevelyan A Memoir (London, 1932), p.124, Sir A E Pease, Elections and Recollections (London, 1932), p.137, Speaker, 1 March 1890, Hanham, Elections and Party Management. p.xv.

155 Lord Askwith, Lord James Of Hereford (London, 1930), p.189.

156 Parry, Rise And Fall Of The Liberal Government, p.307.

Edward Dicey the editor of the Observer, and acknowledged by Gladstone, himself, as a constitutional authority. A V Dicey claimed in a widely acclaimed publication that the Bill was fatally flawed for it would render the sovereignity of the Westminster parliament not only "legally doubtful", but morally unsound" by setting up a separate parliament in Dublin.[157] Such a claim, at the height of the British people's confidence in their imperial destiny and in the superiority of their national institutions, was to be sufficient to outweigh even a measure promoted with all the force of Gladstone's powerful moral and political leadership.

However, the balance of support for the Union within Society and among the intelligentsia does not seem to have been reflected within the Liberal Party in the House of Commons, perhaps an indication that a number of mainstream Liberal MPs supported Home Rule out of loyalty to Gladstone. The majority within the Political Committee of the Reform Club conformed to that of the parliamentary party, as is illustrated at Appendix 4. Given some uncertainty in the case of certain individuals, particularly among those who were never MPs, the Appendix shows a majority of just over two to one in Gladstone's favour, close enough to the majority within the Liberal Party in the House of Commons.[158]

In his closely argued analysis of their voting records, Professor Lubenow found no evidence that division among Liberal MPs over Home Rule had any basis in class. Nor did he conclude that other traditional differences within the 'broad church' of the Party had played any obvious part. In short he concluded that Home Rule was indeed an ideological issue which cut across rather than reinforced the usual political affiliations and compacts.[159] When applied to the context of the membership of London's Liberal clubs, such a conclusion suggests that division over Home Rule was perceived by individuals, at the time and without the benefit of hindsight, as 'artificial' in political terms, and therefore an issue that should not be permitted to threaten the survival of their Club. Thus even the more politically active members on both sides were able to convince themselves that a Unionist was no less a Liberal because he was also a Unionist. Indeed he was to call himself a Liberal Unionist, and was likely to have more in common with his Home Rule colleagues in the Reform Club than he had with members of the Carlton Club. In any case membership of a club was always likely to exercise a moderating influence on opinions, certainly on the expression of those opinions, in the case of all but the most 'unclubbable' of individuals as the

---

157 A V Dicey, England's Case Against Home Rule (London, 1886), pp.251/2.

158 Of the three hundred and thirty-three MPs classed as Liberals, ninety-four voted against and two hundred and twenty-eight, some 70%, for the first Home Rule Bill on second reading. Ten MPs were absent and the Speaker did not declare himself.

159 W C Lubenow, Parliamentary Politics And The Home Rule Crisis (Oxford, 1988), pp.335-339.

history of the Political Committee tends to show.

It follows that two main factors appear to lie behind the successful establishment of a 'modus vivendi' within the Reform Club in spite of the fundamental differences of opinion over Home Rule. First, the traditional dislike of most members for the potential disharmony within the Club provoked by the active pursuit of political initiatives within the 'broad church' of Liberalism. This factor was no doubt allied to a perception of the real threat to the Club's continued existence, to the social status and good living brought about by membership, which 'uncontrolled' blackballing or numerous resignations from either side would bring. Second, a belief among many followers of Gladstone, which Professor Matthew explores in his introduction to Volume X of Gladstone's Diaries, that Home Rule would not bring separatism in its wake but was merely a measure of devolution of local Irish affairs to an Irish Assembly. While it was an action which took into account the historical position of Ireland, and was a matter of practical politics, it was also a thoroughly Liberal measure towards the devolution of responsible local self government similar, if not precisely so, to such as would in due course be brought into effect within the rest of the United Kingdom.[160] Protagonists of Home Rule would have convinced themselves that the 'Split' was a temporary affair, and would have seen the Club as having a major part to play in contributing directly to a resolution of differences through the promotion of discussion and reason in the best traditions of Liberalism.

Professor Lubenow goes on to refer to membership of London clubs as one of three characteristics which served as "indicators of assimilation" among and between MPs, the others being the shared experience of membership of the House of Commons, and similarly of experience in a governing Administration. He also maintains that Home Rule did not "fragment the fundamental basis of parliamentary Liberalism".[161] Admittedly it split the Party sending it into the political wilderness for the best part of twenty years. Certainly public perception of the major division within British politics over much of that period was the issue of Irish Home Rule. However, this was surely a perception inflamed by Gladstone himself in the late 1880s and early 1990s, as he linked Irish injustice with the injustices felt by <u>unskilled</u> workers in Britain now combining for the first time to fight for security of employment and for a decent wage. In other words as he returned to the familiar ground of another moral crusade. Some Liberal Unionists did return to the fold between 1887 and the general election of 1892, while those who prized their Unionism above their Liberalism were only assimilated very slowly into a Conservative and Unionist Party. "Every real Liberal, to whatever section he may belong, clings to the hope that present divisions will

---

160 Matthew, <u>Gladstone Diaries</u>, Vol.X, pp.cxlvi-clx.

161 Lubenow, <u>Parliamentary Politics</u>, pp.272/3 and note 62 on p.272. Among leading Liberals only G J Goschen, who resigned from the Reform Club as early as December 1884, actually joined the Conservative Party.

not be eternal; but that by-and-by 'the flag which is rent in twain, will be one again and without seam'".[162] In a speech to the Unionist Club in March 1894, Sir Henry James was reported to have expressed the hope that Lord Rosebery's succession as leader of the Party might provide a way ahead for the 'return' of Liberal Unionists.[163] It is perhaps only with hindsight that the issue of Irish Home Rule can reasonably be seen as part of the larger debate on the merits of imperialism and the unrelenting advance of democratic pressures. It was indeed an ideological issue in itself, but an element also of a far wider struggle within British politics.

Nevertheless, Liberal political clubs were faced with a serious situation during and immediately after the general election campaign of 1886, and one which the Press was not slow to exploit. As early as the first week in June, even before the vote on Second Reading had destroyed the First Home Rule Bill, the Secretary of the Reform Club published a denial of a report in the Daily Telegraph that candidates opposed to Home Rule were being blackballed. The newspaper was not slow to return to the charge, reinforcing the point of its original disclosure in its carefully worded riposte.

> "Mr Halford and his Committee have misread the paragraph which they contradict. It did not allege that the six Unionist candidates were blackballed for being Unionists but stated the fact that the six rejected were all Unionists, and the six elected of the opposite view."[164]

By the end of June the General Committee had already moved to establish its own impartiality and therefore that of the Club as a whole. A resolution denying that it was a matter on which the Club's ruling committee felt justified in giving advice one way or the other was passed in response to a request by Thomas Kennedy, owner of an engineering company in Leeds, as to whether under the rules of the club "he would be justified in voting against the Party now headed by Mr Gladstone." There is no evidence to suppose that the query was 'planted' by Unionist supporters to force the issue into the open, or was other than a genuine request for elucidation. At the same meeting the General Committee was careful to resolve that the posting of a notice asking for subscriptions from members on behalf of 'Ministerial candidates' should be matched by another on behalf of Liberal Unionist candidates should this be requested.[165]

---

162 Speaker, 1 March 1890, an article under title of 'The Liberal Split And Liberal Clubs'.

163 The Times, 21 March 1894, p.8b. Sir Henry James (1829-1911) was Attorney General in Gladstone's First and Second Administrations and one of three Liberal Unionists (the others being the Duke of Devonshire and Joseph Chamberlain) to serve in Lord Salisbury's Cabinet. A Trustee of the Reform Club, member of its Political Committee from 1887 and one of its two Vice-Chairmen from 1890 until his death in 1911, he was created Baron James of Hereford in 1895.

164 Daily Telegraph 4 and 5 June 1886.

165 Reform Club, GC Minutes, 28 June 1886, PC Minute Book 3, pp.52-58

The Political Committee, not even consulted on Kennedy's request, avoided meeting at all between July 1886 and May 1887, other than at a special meeting to elect a replacement for a member who had died. On 12 June it effectively suspended all elections under Rule IV, following a complaint from one of its own members. James Grahame, the Unionist chairman of the West of Scotland Liberal Association, asserted that the recent election of Herbert Gladstone to the Club had not conformed to the rules of such elections, clearly implying that it had been pushed through with undue haste in order to avoid the risk of blackballing.[166] Grahame had not been present at the meeting which had resolved to elect Herbert Gladstone under Rule IV, although at least three of the fourteen members present were also Unionist supporters. But these were English, and Grahame's strong reaction undoubtedly reflected the domestic struggle among Scottish Liberals. This was to rise to a climax at their annual meeting in October 1887 with a successful resolution calling for Scottish Home Rule. The Scottish, and for that matter Welsh, dimension to Irish Home Rule emphasises the complexity of the issues, not only those concerned with the maintenance of the integrity and unity of the United Kingdom and its Imperial (and English) Parliament at Westminster, but also those concerned with the land. Land, as always, was a central issue in the struggle for Irish self determination at any level. There were major concerns in Scotland as well as in England over 'buying out' Irish landlords with British taxpayers' money, and the implications of such an action for the relationship between landlord and tenant throughout the United Kingdom. Grahame kept up the pressure, following discussion of the possibility of renewing elections under Rule IV in 1890, by proposing that these should not take place "unless for services [to the Liberal cause] antecedent to the period of our unhappy differences".[167] Elections under the Rule were not re-instated until 1892, and then broadly on the basis of electing one candidate from 'each side'.

The experience of other Liberal clubs was broadly similar to that of the Reform. A spate of blackballing, which in the circumstances must be construed as having a political basis, accompanied by speculation in the Press about the "possible destruction" of famous clubs. This would be followed by the resignations of some individuals, and then by the recognition of wiser counsel leading to an uneasy 'truce' and the suspension of active political initiatives on the part of the individual club. At Brooks's allegedly offensive remarks by Sir William Harcourt are reported to have led to the blackballing of his son, Lewis, by angry Unionists. Reprisals followed with, most notably, the same treatment being meted out to William Palmer, the son of a former

166 <u>Herbert John Gladstone</u> *(1854-1930). Fourth son of the Right Honourable William Ewart Gladstone. Liberal Chief Whip 1899-1905. Home Secretary December 1905-February 1910, when he was appointed Governor of South Africa and created Viscount Gladstone. A member of the Political Committee of the Reform Club from 1900 and a Vice-Chairman of that Committee from 1906 to 1929.*

167 *Reform Club, PC Minute Book 3, p.74.*

Liberal Lord Chancellor, the now Unionist Lord Selborne. For a while it seemed that reason and civilised conduct were in danger even in the stronghold of Whiggism. "It looked as though nobody would be elected except an occasional whist-player who detested politics".[168] Ultimately the normal atmosphere of Brooks's was only restored through the "matchless powers of persuasion" and vast spread of "cousinship across all parties" of Lord Granville.[169]

Only at the National Liberal Club, among the capital's residential as opposed to purely dining clubs such as the Eighty, Articles and Radical Clubs, did events subsequently take a more permanently acrimonious turn. Here a large number of Liberal Unionist resignations occurred in January 1889, the Liberal and Radical in particular revelling in the opportunity to 'rub salt in the wound'. "Mr Chamberlain went some time ago, and the departure of the rest of 'the Tory crutch' will probably do the club a service. . . The Political Committee of the club now has an opportunity of showing its ability. It has never had a fair field up to this time; so the sooner we hear its policy the better".[170] The membership of the National Liberal Club, whose rules stated firmly that a member had to be a Liberal in politics, went on to rescind a resolution of 1887 that it was no longer desirable for the Club to take an active part in politics. By this action the Club effectively confirmed its 'takeover' of the active, as opposed perhaps to purely symbolic, political leadership of Liberal clubs from the Reform. Provincial constituency associations had always been well represented among its membership. Following defeat of the First Home Rule Bill, and with the notable exception of 'Joseph Chamberlain's Birmingham', these rallied to Gladstone under the banner of the National Liberal Federation while younger Liberals and Radicals went on to play an increasingly large part in the National Liberal Club's affairs. The Radical Henry Labouchere's election to the chairmanship of the General Committee of that Club in May 1897 confirmed a trend already in existence for some years.[171] Nevertheless, it would be wrong to assume that all Liberal Unionists had resigned from the National Liberal Club by the end of 1889. Some remained, most notably Sir Henry James.

---

168 James Pope-Hennessy, Lord Crewe 1858:1945 The Likeness Of A Liberal (London, 1955), pp.16/17. This recollection of Lord Crewe, who became Chairman of the Political Committee of the Reform Club in 1929, is noted by Professor Lubenow who also details other references describing this incident. See Lubenow, Parliamentary Politics, p.278 and notes 80 and 81. However, the Leeds Mercury found alternative explanations for the blackballing at Brooks's, citing a dinner for Gladstone construed as a 'political banquet' by Liberal Unionists, and the 'treatment' (not specified) meted out to Sir Horace Davey. See Leeds Mercury, 11 and 15 February 1887.

169 Southgate, Passing Of The Whigs, p.342.

170 Liberal and Radical, 12 January 1889.

171 National Liberal Club, SGM Minutes, 8 December 1887 and 1 May 1889, GC Minutes, 20 February 1889.

In The Wake Of The First Home Rule Bill

No direct reference to the understanding reached within the Reform Club can be gleaned from the minutes of its Committees at the time. The <u>Leeds Mercury</u> referred to suspension of ballots for membership in an article in early February 1887, while emphasising that these had now re-started and no cases of blackballing of Unionists or Home Rulers had occurred at the most recent ballot. <u>The Times</u> wrote of a spirit of tolerance or indifference at the Club which had replaced that of its former "pugnacious political nature... The Reform grows less uncompromising in its Liberalism."[172] Apparently leading Conservatives were invited, and came, to the Club's Jubilee Ball.[173] However, there are a number of letters written in the decades following the 'Split' which have survived in the Club's archive. From these it is clear that a "modus vivendi" was reached with some rapidity following the general election of July 1886. Among the more interesting are two letters on the subject of the vacant chairmanship of the Political Committee. These were written following the death of Charles Villiers in 1898, no less than twelve years after the defeat of the First Home Rule Bill in the Commons and some four years after the Lords had 'killed' a second Bill. Extracts from both are quoted below, the first written by the then Chairman of the General Committee to Sir Henry James, by then Lord James of Hereford and a member of Lord Salisbury's Cabinet:

> ". . . The possibility of your nomination to the post now vacant was discussed at a meeting of the General Committee some weeks ago, at which as it happened the majority of the members present belonged to the Unionist section of the Liberal party. The Committee was absolutely unanimous in the opinion that the election of a member of Lord Salisbury's Cabinet as chairman of the Pol. Com. would be most disastrous to the interests of the Club . . . All who are concerned in its management have done their utmost since 1886 to prevent friction between the two sections of the party. . . The maintenance of the status quo which has hitherto guided the political committee in its actions since 1886 seems to me and the General Committee to be the only mode of avoiding a rupture that would cause incalculable harm to the Club. . . If I might venture to make a personal suggestion it would be that the Pol. Com. should leave matters as at present, with yourself and Sir Joseph Pease [supporter of Home Rule] as Vice Chairmen the Chairmanship being left unfilled. . ."

Lord James reacted swiftly, his letter to the Secretary of the Political Committee dated three days later:

---

172 Leeds Mercury, 11 February 1887, The Times, 16 June 1887, p.6a. Of the four MPs who were elected and the subject of the article in the Leeds Mercury, Robert Wallace and Sydney Buxton were Home Rulers and R Verdin and WP Sinclair were Unionists.

173 Hamilton, Parliamentary Reminiscences, Vol.2, p.75.

"... I must think of the interests of the Reform Club – and I must not be unmindful of the natural feelings of every section of its members. I also am very desirous to assist in maintaining the modus vivendi arrived at in 1886. I certainly can do nothing to endanger it. . . I have come to the conclusion that I must ask you to be good enough not to place me in nomination for that office."

These two extracts provide an insight into the political framework of the Reform Club between 1886 and the end of the century.[174] They indicate that by mutual agreement the General and Political Committees continued to be composed of both Gladstonians and Liberal Unionists, with the latter still considered to be a 'section of the Liberal Party'. They prove the existence of a formal understanding reached in 1886, making clear its prolonged and delicate nature. They confirm the recognition by both sides that it would be disastrous for the Club if that understanding was upset, even by the assumption of an appointment which had been little more than symbolic for over a decade.

It is claimed that evidence of the strong feelings which still lay beneath the surface was provided by the reaction to a request by one hundred and twenty-five members for a subscription list to be placed on the Club table towards the commissioning of a portrait of Gladstone. A number of members questioned the partisanship of such a list at that particular time, which provoked the General Committee into taking similar action for the commissioning of a portrait of the Unionist Lord Hartington.[175] Much has been made by the Club's historian of Sir Henry Lucy's account of the 'great portrait race', as first one and then the other list took the lead until finally there was hardly a guinea difference between the two contributions. It is true that subscriptions for each list were limited to one guinea per member and confined to members of the Club, although some individuals did contribute to both lists. Both men were held in high regard but Lucy also maintains that while Hartington sat for his portrait, Gladstone apparently declined to reciprocate, forcing the Club to 'pick up' a "melancholy, almost unrecognisable likeness" elsewhere.[176] However significant the portrait race may have been, evidence of those strong feelings and of the fragility of the prolonged understanding between the two sides is perhaps better indicated by two other sources. First, the continuing annual resolution to leave the chairmanship of the Political Committee vacant between 1898 and 1911 when it was to be filled by no less a figure than the Prime Minister, Herbert Asquith. Second, the contents of some of the letters which have survived in the Club's archive.

---

174 (Thomas) Wemyss Reid to Lord James of Hereford, 25 February 1898, Lord James of Hereford to Frank Finlay, 28 February 1898, Reform Club mss., Box. 9.

175 Reform Club, GC Minutes, 20 January 1888. See also The Times, 21 January 1898, p.6a, which refers to the membership's decision to hang both portraits in the dining room.

176 Lucy, A Diary Of The Salisbury Parliament, p.514, Woodbridge, Reform Club, pp.32/33.

Such correspondence includes a letter from a prominent Liberal Unionist member of the General Committee declining to attend a particular dinner, for "every one who dines will be deemed to be tarred with the Gladstonian Brush."[177] Election of the Party's principal organiser, Francis Schnadhorst, to the Club under Rule IV in March 1893 gave rise to some ill feeling, although it is a little difficult in his case to separate social distaste from that of politics, Schnadhorst being a 'paid official' of the Party! Nevertheless, Schnadhorst was at the forefront of the successful move to swing the Party's organisation behind Home Rule, and is likely to have made Liberal Unionist enemies in the process. Sir Henry James wrote to the Secretary of the Political Committee regretting his inability to find a Unionist to put up with Schnadhorst for all were unwilling to be "bracketted" with him. It was also in April 1893 that James informed the Secretary of his certainty that Joseph Chamberlain would not accept re-election to the Reform Club by the Political Committee, possibly also a part of the search for a Unionist.[178] The issue of Chamberlain's re-election was raised again in 1896, this time by the same staunch Liberal Unionist, James Grahame, who had been opposed to further use of Rule IV in 1887 and 1890. He wrote that he would continue to oppose elections under the Rule, unless one Unionist and one supporter of Home Rule were always put up and elected 'in tandem'. But he went on to say that it would prejudice the "dignity of the Club" to re-elect Chamberlain unless he specifically requested re-election. "I will not support him for special election unless he makes the amende honourable to the Club – whose dust he cast of[f] his shoes".[179] Such a public attitude towards Chamberlain as early as 1893, from another firm Liberal Unionist, provides further confirmation that many members placed the wellbeing of Club before politics. Grahame relaxed his attitude on Rule IV some days later, agreeing exceptionally to the election of the Marquis of Crewe even if the Committee failed to find a Liberal Unionist to elect with him.[180]

In early 1899, some eight months after Gladstone's death, the Chairman of the General Committee expressed "grave doubts" over a proposal that "the Gladstonian party" should hold their forthcoming meeting to elect a new leader on the Club's premises. His letter shows the continuing strong, even unbalanced, feelings on the issue of Home Rule among the membership. It emphasises the potentially disastrous effect on the recruitment of new members of any perceived partisanship on the part of the ruling committee, and the determination of that committee to put the interests of Club before those of politics:

---

177 Marston Buszard to Frederick Inderwick, 20 April 1887, Reform Club mss., Box 9.

178 James to Finlay, 12 and 18 April 1893, Reform Club mss., Box 9.

179 Grahame to Finlay, 2 February 1896, Reform Club mss., Box 9.

180 Grahame to Finlay, 6 February 1896, Reform Club mss., Box 9.

"... I think the proposal made last week to open the Club for the purpose of the meeting savours somewhat of partisanship. The Unionist party, at the present time, are not in a position in which it would be practicable for us to make them a similar offer . . . I fear that many [candidates for membership] may think the club labelled "Gladstonian" after such a meeting and withdraw their names . . . The paucity of names in the candidates book has been for some time a matter of anxiety. Personally I think it is unreasonable to have an objection to the proposed meeting but we represent many unreasonable people, and we come back to the only profitable question – whether in the opinion of the Committee such a meeting is or is not for the benefit of the club? . . ."[181]

On 6 February 1899 the meeting did take place and in the Smoking Room. One hundred and forty-three Liberal MPs elected Sir Henry Campbell-Bannerman as leader of the Liberal Party in the House of Commons. The decision, however reluctant, to allow the Club's premises to be used in this way, suggests that the Reform Club continued to be seen at least as a symbol of Liberalism, whatever the scale of its absence from active party politics. The Club had been a natural choice of meeting place for Liberals to elect their leader since Gladstone's first resignation in 1875. Campbell-Bannerman had made clear his determination to hold the meeting of 6 February 1899 there. In a letter to Herbert Asquith he wrote:

". . . my disposition is all for the Reform Club. Anything else would be a confession of weakness. . . Why should we lose our hold on so excellent a property? And as a matter of fact I believe more of our men (certainly the best of them) belong to it than to any other. To go to another Club would be a slap on the cheek of the Reform, and we should get all our men blackballed. . ."[182]

In July 1901 he chose the Club to seek and obtain his vote of confidence from Liberal MPs, following the uproar stemming from his 'methods of barbarism' speech on the South African War; although not, it should be added, without strongly worded protests, and even a number of resignations, from anti-Radical and anti-Boer members of the Club.[183] On 30 April 1908 Herbert Asquith also used the Reform Club for the meeting which confirmed his election as leader and Prime Minister. It was in this speech he referred to

---

181 *Walter Macnamara to Malcolm Morris, 17 January 1899, Reform Club mss., Box 9.*

182 *Sir Henry Campbell-Bannerman to Herbert Asquith, 17 January 1899, AP, Bodleian Library, ms. 9, ff.167-169. See also P Stansky,* <u>Ambitions and Strategies: The Struggle for Leadership of the Liberal Party in the 1890s</u> *(Oxford, 1964), p.287.*

183 *A spate of resignations occurred in late 1901/early 1902, no doubt of members whose imperialist sympathies left them feeling out of place. Their complaints are summed up in three letters from a Mr Hutton to the Club's Secretary in the Club's archive. See Richard Hutton to William Newbigging, 9 December 1901, 3 March and 11 April 1902, Reform Club mss., Box 9. See also* <u>The Times</u>, *8 and 9 July 1901, pp.6f and 11f.*

the right of Liberal MPs, notwithstanding the prerogative of the Sovereign, "to determine who the Liberal leader shall be".[184] On 8 December 1916 he summoned members of both Houses of Parliament there, effectively to obtain a vote of confidence in his continuing leadership of the Liberal Party, following his decision to resign as Prime Minister in favour of David Lloyd George. This was the last large scale political meeting of Liberal MPs to be held at the Reform Club. Their resolution to support Lloyd George's government, while at the same time pledging support for Asquith as leader of the Party, has been described by one prominent modern historian as the moment when the "two versions of true Liberalism parted company", and by another as the moment when the "old Liberal party . . . was dispersing for ever".[185]

Meanwhile a beleaguered General Committee, apparently neither consulting nor being consulted by the Political Committee which was only meeting some twice a year at this stage, found little relief from the onerous business of trying to keep politics in the background of the Club's affairs. The bitter division among Liberals over the conduct of the war in South Africa added to their problems. In a letter Sir John Wolfe-Barry asked for clarification on the role of the Political Committee, commenting that he would only join the Club providing it meant that he was not "even indirectly supposed to support Home Rule or pro Boer politicians". The Club's Secretary replied the same day that he understood the Political Committee was careful to ensure a balance within its own membership. He went on to say:

> ". . . there is no Chairman but two Vice Chairmen one of each party . . . They take no part in political matters at all but sometimes under the rules elect a couple of members – one of each party. . ."[186]

Several letters addressed to the Club's Chairman in early March 1904 testify to the anger felt by Liberal Unionist members at an accusation levelled against a candidate for membership, Sir Hugh Smiley, that he was Chairman of the Paisley Conservative Association. These use such expressions as 'malicious falsehood', while emphasising Sir Hugh's appointments as Chairman of the Paisley Liberal Unionist Association and Vice President of the West of Scotland and of the Ulster Liberal Unionist Associations. Again the Political Committee seems not to have been involved at all. It failed to meet at all between March 1903 and June 1905, when its attention had to be drawn by the General Committee to the number of vacancies in its ranks including that of Secretary – as well as Chairman!

---

184 Liberal Magazine, Vol. XVI, May 1908, p.230.

185 Michael Bentley, The Climax Of Liberal Politics: British Liberalism In Theory And Practice 1868-1918 (London, 1987), p.148, Trevor Wilson, Downfall of the Liberal Party (London, 1966), p.101.

186. Sir John Wolfe-Barry to Newbigging, 6 December 1901. Newbigging to Wolfe-Barry, 6 December 1901, Reform Club mss., Box 9. Wolfe-Barry joined the Club in 1902.

5 A REVISED ROLE AND A CHANGING MEMBERSHIP

Dinners 'Of A Political Character'

Moves by Asquith's Liberal government towards the introduction of a third Home Rule Bill gave rise to the last 'flurry' of surviving correspondence in the Reform Club's archive associated with the 'Split'. In November 1911 the Political Committee found its voice again with a proposal that the Prime Minister, elected to the Club under Rule IV by the Committee some nineteen years before, should be invited to fill the vacant chairmanship. The invitation can be seen as part of an effort to rally support for Asquith's leadership in the face of renewed bitterness arising from parliamentary clashes on such ideological issues as the powers of the House of Lords, Disestablishment and Free Trade. It can also be seen as a move to encourage support for the introduction of a third Home Rule Bill now that the powers of the House of Lords had been restricted by the Parliament Act.[187] Asquith replied that he would be happy to accept "on the understanding that no active work will be expected in connection with the position".[188]

That invitation to Asquith was preceded in the Spring by two letters which could be said to have been the spur which galvanised the Committee into a renewal of open political activity. The first was written by Mr Lionel Robinson, a Liberal Unionist recently elected to the Political Committee, in which he accused the Committee of irrelevance and went on to allege that some of its members were meeting in private to promote political programmes of their own. He claimed that:

> "...it [the Political Committee] no longer - so far as was known to its members as a body, performed any function which could be called even by courtesy - political . . . I fail to see the value of keeping up the pretence of an openly elected committee (for specific objects) which does absolutely nothing, while an unknown and self-constituted body does take an active part in political work: and keeps its proceedings secret..." [189]

The second letter, from a Mr George Holford Knight, proposed a review of the desirability of holding regular dinners of a political character.[190] Perhaps unsurprisingly, there is no mention of Robinson's letter in the minutes, nor is

---

187 *The Parliament Act became law in August 1911. The Third Home Rule Bill was introduced on 11 April 1912.*

188 *Asquith to Sir William Collins, 15 November 1911, Reform Club mss., Box 9.*

189. *Lionel Robinson to Political Committee Secretary (Sir William Collins), 20 April [1911], Reform Club mss., box 9. Although no year has been added to the date, references within the letter make it quite clear that the year was 1911.*

190 *Reform Club, PC Minute Book 3, p.186. Holford Knight became a parliamentary candidate for the Labour Party in 1922, and was ultimately elected under the banner of National Labour at the general election of October 1931.*

there any trace of other references to 'committees within committees'. However, support for Holford Knight's proposal was immediate. This took the form of a recommendation that the Political Committee should be permitted to institute a series of regular dinners for leading members of the Liberal Party, at which discussion upon political subjects of current interest would be invited. The General Committee agreed with some caution to participate in a joint sub-committee to examine the implications. Three months later, and shortly after Asquith's acceptance of the chairmanship of the Political Committee, formal agreement was given on the understanding that such occasions were private affairs, that is to say confined to members of the Political Committee and their guests, and held in the Strangers Room.[191]

Use of the dining facilities of the Reform Club as a way of showing respect and support for prominent public figures from home and abroad, with whom Reformers or Liberals could identify, was an important part of the Club's tradition. Most notably, in the years before the Split of 1886, banquets had been held for such distinguished foreigners as Ibrahim Pasha of Egypt (1846), like his father Mehemet Ali 'a hammer of the Turk' and renowned for welcoming Western European travellers to his dominions, for Garibaldi (1864), and for Ulysees C Grant (1877). Periodic dinners for distinguished home-grown Liberals included one for Lord Palmerston (1850), significantly at the time of his difference of opinion over Balkan policy with the Whig leadership of the Party, for the elderly Radical Admiral Sir Charles Napier (1854), before he sailed in command of the Baltic fleet as part of the offensive against Russia, for the Earl of Dufferin (1879), following the period of his governor generalship of Canada, for Sir Henry Campbell-Bannerman (1884), and for Sir Charles Dilke (1885).

The separate issue of holding <u>regular</u> 'dinners of a political character' had first been raised in the middle of the crisis leading up to the vote on Second Reading of the First Home Rule Bill. A formal motion in favour was carried at a Special General Meeting of the Club on 20 May 1886. The motion was not taken up until the following year, no doubt in the light of the controversy over the Home Rule Bill. It was then raised again as part of a proposal for a programme to popularise the Club in the light of a dwindling candidates' list, and in anticipation of the need to hold a function to commemorate the Club's Golden Jubilee. After much deliberation it was agreed by the Political Committee that no functions at all of a political nature should be recommended, but that the General Committee should be advised that some form of non-political event should be arranged for the Jubilee. On 19 May 1888, reflecting concern that any function at all at this time might be misrepresented as an example of partisanship, the General Committee baulked even at that suggestion, but ultimately agreed providing that it

---

191 *Reform Club, PC Minute Book 3, pp.192 and 198, GC Minutes, 16 and 23 November 1911 and 18 February 1912. Correspondence between Political and General Committees, and the report of the sub-committee recommending the institution of regular political dinners, are contained in the Club's archive. See Reform Club mss. Box 9.*

received a formal requisition, and a Jubilee Ball was held on 20 June. Although the custom of giving periodic Club dinners for prominent individuals continued, the subject of holding regular dinners of a political character under the auspices of the Political Committee seems to have been allowed to drop.[192]

Even as late as 1911 a strong reaction to any decision permitting the Political Committee to renew any form of active role was always likely, particularly in association with a Liberal government's attempt to introduce yet another Home Rule Bill. Meetings of the General Committee on 21 December 1911 and 11 January 1912 record the resignations of some thirty members, perhaps as many as might have been expected from the declining rump of Unionists still associated with the Liberal Party. The few surviving letters, which include two dated later in 1912, refer to anger at the end of the 'truce' of 1886. They threaten resistance to the use of the Club for furthering the 'disastrous' policy of Home Rule. They accuse the Political Committee of partisanship, and they point to the revolutionary policies of the present Liberal government including "destruction of the unity of the Kingdom and Empire".[193] The issue was put most directly by Marston Buszard in a letter to the Chairman of the General Committee in mid December 1911:

> "...I hear rumours that an attempt is to be made to make the Club the centre of active and public propagandism of Home Rule Principles without regard to the feelings of the very considerable number of members who regard these principles as destructive to the well-being of the Country. If this is so, I imagine that those of us who are anti-Home Rulers will no longer be able to remain members of the Club. . . From the appearance of the Candidates Book the Club appears none too prosperous...Of course it is a high honour to have the Prime Minister of the day Chairman of the Political Committee, but I do not see that this fact need alter the terms on which the Club has been carried on for the last twenty five years. . . "[194]

That third attempt by a Liberal government to resolve the issue of Irish self determination, thrown into sharper focus from 1912 by a militant Ulster, was to be overtaken by a World War and drag on through the years of that war and into the future. It rates little more than an isolated mention in the surviving correspondence of the Reform Club from that time.

192 Reform Club, PC Minute Book 3, p.70.

193 Robert McCall to Macnamara, 28 December 1911, Charles Graves to Macnamara, 5 January 1912, Thomas Lauder Brunton to Newbigging, 26 October 1912, Thomas Russell to Club Secretary, 12 November 1912, Reform Club mss., Box 9. McCall did not, but Graves, Lauder Brunton and Thomas Russell were among those who did resign from the Club.

194 Marston Buszard to Macnamara, 12 December 1911, Reform Club mss., Box 9. In spite of his strong language, Buszard does not seem to have carried out his threat to resign.

With the exception of the years of the war and its immediate aftermath - the Political Committee did not meet at all between March 1915 and March 1920 - dinners of a political character were held regularly from 1912, their organisation and direction apparently becoming the major raison d'etre for the Political Committee's continued existence. Appropriately the first of these, on 19 March 1912, was held in honour of the Committee's new Chairman, and others followed. A dinner was held for him in 1920, one on being created Earl of Oxford and Asquith in 1925, and another the following year on his resignation as leader of the Liberal Party. It follows that Lloyd George was never similarly treated, although it is alleged that a proposal for the Club itself to hold a dinner in his honour in 1910 was allowed to drop by the General Committee.[195] A number of other leading Liberals accepted invitations to dinner from the Political Committee. Most notably these included Sir Edward Grey in 1912, the Marquis of Crewe on his appointment as HM Ambassador in Paris in 1923, Sir Herbert Samuel following return from his appointment as High Commissioner in Palestine in 1927, and Sir John Simon at the conclusion of the work of the Indian Statutory Commission in 1930. It was Sir Herbert Samuel who suggested broadening the scope of such dinners to include individuals from outside politics. His proposal, subsequently approved by the General Committee, led to the holding of two very successful banquets in 1928, on behalf of the Club as a whole, for representatives of Literature, Science and Philosophy (the "Intelligentsia") and for those from Commerce and Industry, who "were of Reform sympathies".[196] Dinners were also held for prominent individuals from outside politics who were "identified with traditional liberalism in its broadest aspect".[197]

The growing sensitivity of many traditional Liberals to any open association with the politics of a divided Liberal Party, about to suffer a further major split into three electoral factions, is illustrated by one exchange of letters in the Spring of 1931. It seems probable that the reservations expressed on this occasion were heightened by the continuing use of the word 'Political' in the title of the Reform Club's principal organising body for functions. An invitation to a recently retired senior judicial figure, Sir Robert Wallace, was met by a tentative acceptance but also a firm request for reassurance:

---

195 Woodbridge, *Reform Club*, p.25.

196 *Reform Club PC Minute Book 3*, p.298. For the first time the speeches were printed, for use by the Liberal Publications Department at that Department's expense. A number of documents referring to these banquets have survived, including the original report of the dinner sub-committee set up to examine Samuel's proposal, and copies of both draft and final lists of guests. See Reform Club mss., Box 9. The two banquets were arranged jointly by the General and Political Committees and held in the Coffee Room.

197 H A L Fisher to Collins, 26 and 31 May 1934, and other correspondence, Reform Club mss., Box 9. Fisher had been an MP between 1916 and 1918.

"...But I wish to be quite candid with you. Is there anything political in it? For the 24 years during which I was Chairman of London Sessions I have never said a word publicly on politics and as an old liberal I am entirely opposed to the action of the official leaders of the liberal party in keeping the Socialist Government in power, which I think is destroying liberalism in the country as all recent elections show. . ."

In spite of assurances of the (by now) non-party political nature of such dinners, including the names of previous distinguished guests from the Diplomatic Service, and a guarantee that the proceedings would be in private with no reporters present, Wallace withdrew his acceptance although ostensibly on the grounds of ill health.[198]

A large number of documents concerned with dinners sponsored by the Political Committee have survived in the Club's archive. These include copies of menus, draft and printed guest lists, and seating plans. Letters include several invitations and their associated acceptances/rejections. These range from Sir Edward Grey's invitation, which included a guarantee that: ". . . no reporters will be present and no formal speeches are expected", to that of a member declining to attend the dinner for Asquith in 1926: ". . . I rejoice to think he has retired from the so-called leadership of the Liberal Party. . . he should never have entered into politics; he is not a Statesman, but he is a great lawyer. . . " Another from Herbert (by then Viscount) Gladstone declined the chair at the dinner for Samuel: " . . . I have so many doubts and misgivings on the present position of the party that I feel unable to make any adequate speech. . ." Yet another from Samuel himself, timed at 7.30 pm, regretted that he was tied up at the House of Commons with "The Lords amendments to the Coal Mines Bill", and would not after all be able to attend the dinner that evening (9 July 1930) for Sir John Simon.[199]

Continuation of the General Committee's cautious approach to its involvement in any function, which might be represented as showing political partisanship, extended even to a proposal from the Political Committee that both committees should co-operate in arrangements for the commemoration of the centenary of the Great Reform Act. On 22 January 1932 the General Committee's response, following consideration of the matter for some six months, was expressed by its Chairman as follows:

"That having given the matter careful consideration the Committee came unanimously to the conclusion that on the whole it is undesirable that it should officially take any part in the celebration of the Centenary of the passing of the Reform Act...on the other hand there would seem to be no objection whatever to the Political Committee itself, if so minded, organising a dinner or some other function. . . "

---

198 *Sir Robert Wallace to Collins, 13 March 1931, Collins to Wallace, 15 March 1931, Wallace to Collins, 19 March 1931. Reform Club mss., Box 9.*

199 *Collins to Sir Edward Grey, 19 June 1912, Sir Leonard Powell to Collins, 30 November 1926, Viscount Gladstone to Collins, 29 April 1927, Sir Herbert Samuel to Collins, 9 July 1930, Reform Club mss., Box 9.*

In the event, and with the General Committee's authority, a banquet was held in the Coffee Room on 7 June 1932, the anniversary of the date on which the Great Reform Act had received the Royal Assent. One hundred and ten attended. The cost was thirty shillings a head. The Marquis of Crewe, as Chairman of the Political Committee, presided. Professor G M Trevelyan, who delivered an oration on the "historical aspects of the Great Reform Bill", and H A L Fisher, Warden of New College Oxford, were among guests of the Committee. Interestingly, it seems that a letter of regret for absence was received from David Lloyd George.[200]

A Changing Membership

This continuing, even growing, sensitivity on the part of the General Committee to any hint of political partisanship on behalf of the Club reflected a changing membership, as well as divisions within the Liberal Party. In his history of the Reform Club, George Woodbridge describes the extent of change in the occupations of members throughout its history. He emphasises the early predominance of members of the legal profession, the decline in the number of serving MPs, the presence among the membership from the start of a large number of "business men", and the more recent rise in the number of members from the growing "public services".[201] Such changes were reflected in the composition of the Political Committee but, unsurprisingly in a Committee dubbed 'Political' of however 'passive' a nature, seem to have taken longer to come about. Admittedly the number of serving MPs continued to dwindle, but it was not until well after the Second World War that individuals with experience of the House of Commons virtually disappeared from its ranks.

Analysis of the membership of the Political Committee shows that Radicals remained in a minority throughout its early years. While their proportionate strength grew and the quality of their MPs improved during the 1870s, numbers fell back quite sharply in the early 1880s. Of the total of fifteen Radicals in the original Committee (see Appendix 2), seven 'Palmerstonian Radicals' had dropped out by 1881, of whom only Thomas Milner Gibson might be said to have been of real political quality. Their 'replacements' included A J Mundella (1874), although he remained a member for less than five years, Sir Charles Dilke (1875), Leonard Courtney (1878), and the great John Bright himself (1878), of whom all were noted for the independence of their Radicalism and chosen to serve in one or more of Gladstone's Cabinets. These were joined by such firm Radical MPs as Edward Jenkins (1870), David Wedderburn (1871), James Barclay (1872),

---

200 Draft report of the Sub-Committee, undated. The proof copy of a volume commemorating the banquet, which includes a record of speeches, is also held in the Club's archive. See Reform Club, mss., Box 9 and PC Minute Book 3, pp.347-350.

201 Woodbridge, Reform Club. pp. 16 and 18.

W E Briggs (1874), James Harrison (1876), and Peter Rylands (1879). In numerical terms fifteen Radicals had grown to eighteen by 1881 but dropped back to thirteen by the time Gladstone formed his Third Administration in 1886. The combined total for mainstream Liberal and Whig MPs, numbering twenty-five members in 1869, also fell over the same period to seventeen. Thus there was a trend within both Club and Committee towards a membership less related to active membership of the House of Commons. This acted further against Radical interests as few non-MPs on the Committee tended to be of that persuasion. A growing disillusionment with the will of existing institutions at the centre of the Party's organisation to support really progressive policies no doubt played a part in these changes. Thus the redeployment of Radical effort at the constituency level through the National Liberal Federation from 1877, and the founding of the National Liberal Club in 1882.

A selection of some key years within the fortunes of the Liberal Party, together with two selected at random from the post-1945 era, shows the scale of the decline in the numbers of serving MPs within the Political Committee, although there were years, for example 1932, when the level of representation temporarily improved. It should be noted that the particularly sharp fall in 1886 also reflects the loss of Liberal seats at the general election of that year:

Year		MPs in Political Committee
1869	First complete year of Gladstone's 1st Administration	40
1881	First complete year of Gladstone's 2nd Administration	36
1885	End of Gladstone's 2nd Administration	32
1886	Following the election fought on the issue of Home Rule	23
1894	Gladstone's final retirement. Rosebery's Administration	14
1906	Return of Liberals with an overall majority of eighty-four	10
1924	Following the 'Red Letter' General Election	9
1930	Following 1929 general election fought under Lloyd George	8
1948	Selected at random from the post-1945 era	5
1967	Selected at random from the post-1945 era	1

However, examination of the numbers of ex-MPs who were still members shows that the Reform Club maintained a traditional, if from 1886 largely symbolic, place at the heart of political Liberalism at least until well after the Second World War. A glance at the membership of the Political Committee as late as 1948 shows that the five MPs shown in the table against that year were accompanied by a further seventeen who had at one time been members of the House of Commons. Of that total of twenty-two, thirteen were Liberals (although one joined the Labour Party that year), a further eight had been Liberals but were now Liberal-Nationalists or Liberal-Conservatives, and one was an Irish Nationalist turned Independent. By 1967 the figures had changed more dramatically, with the one (Liberal) MP shown in the table accompanied by just one ex-MP, and he had represented a Labour seat.

Many key political figures within the organisation of the Party after 1886 accepted election to the Political Committee. Most Liberal Chief Whips were members, including Arnold Morley (1885), Herbert Gladstone (1900), Alexander Murray, Master of Elibank (1911), P H Illingworth (1912), Henry Vivian Phillips (1923), Sir Robert Hutchison (1927), Walter Rea (1933), and P A Harris (1922). All these were members during all or part of their retention of the appointment.[202] F E Guest was elected to the Committee, but not until November 1922, that is to say immediately after he had vacated the appointment of Chief Whip for the Liberals supporting Lloyd George's Coalition government.[203] Between 1937 and 1940 the Chief Whips of both the 'official' Liberal Parliamentary Party and those Liberals describing themselves as National Liberals, respectively P A Harris (1922) and Charles Iain Kerr (1932), were simultaneously members of the Political Committee. Harris remained Chief Whip of the former until 1945.

The absence of an active party political role on the part of the Committee may have contributed to the credibility of such arrangements. Election to membership no doubt continued to add to individual status, and provided an opportunity to keep a finger on the pulse of influential Liberal thinking, of whatever leaning. This is borne out by the number of Liberal Cabinet Ministers who also continued to accept election, although many did so following their period of office, and few ever attended a meeting either in or out of office. Those Cabinet Ministers between 1887 and 1937, who were simultaneously members of the Political Committee, included Sir Henry Campbell-Bannerman (1877), Arnold Morley (1885), Lord James of Hereford (1892), Marquis of Crewe (1897), Herbert Gladstone (1900), Herbert Asquith (1911), John Seely (1911), T McKinnon Wood (1915), Walter Runciman (1917), Sir Donald Maclean (1918), Sir Herbert Samuel (1920), Sir John Simon (1920), Marquis of Reading (1931), and Sir Archibald Sinclair (1932).[204]

Such a parade of Liberal talent tends to obscure the growing weakness of the links between Liberal Party (or Parties) and Club, if not necessarily between Club and a traditional Liberal ethos. Division among Liberals may once again have been put aside to rally the Party under the banner of Free Trade before the general election of 1906. However, by 1911, with the Reform Club embarked at last on the process of purging itself of the issue of Home Rule for Ireland, other differences had already been apparent for some time at the heart of the Liberal Administration. These were ultimately to sow

---

202 *Years in brackets show year of first election to the Political Committee. Individuals are only listed with titles if these were held at the time of that election.*

203. *Guest joined the Conservative Party in 1930 and sat as a Conservative MP from 1931 to 1937. He resigned from the Reform Club as early as 1925.*

204 *Dates in brackets show the year of first election to the Political Committee. Individuals are listed with the titles held by them as Cabinet Ministers.*

an even more bitter harvest than Home Rule, and to prove disastrous for the fortunes of a parliamentary party already weakened by the electoral success of forty Labour candidates at the general election of January 1910, and by Labour gains in local elections. There is no doubt that, as an issue, Home Rule was part of a wider ideological struggle within the Liberal Party over the nature and importance of empire, and of democracy itself. But the pursuit of Home Rule also seems to have been used by many leading Liberals, even after Gladstone's death, as an excuse for failure to grasp the nettle of social reform. In a new biography of Sir Charles Dilke, David Nicholls emphasises the unchanging social composition of the Liberal Party in the years before the Great War. More importantly, by reference to the election manifestos of Liberal candidates at the general election of 1906, he shows the preponderance of traditional issues such as Home Rule, Temperance, Disestablishment, Free Trade and reform of Education. He goes on to contrast these with those 'new' issues important to the growing political power of organised labour: more representation in parliament by the working class, steps to combat unemployment, rights of trade unions, and the campaign for old age pensions.[205]

The loss of Joseph Chamberlain, over Home Rule in 1886, may well have played a significant part in the slow progress made by traditional Liberalism in adapting itself to the changing political scene and the demands of a growing democracy. Yet Conservative political leadership between 1886 and 1906, based on the traditional governing class, was bolstered by its 'alliance' with the Radical, Unionist and later, imperialist Joseph Chamberlain.

> "Had there been no Home Rule split and had he [Chamberlain] succeeded Gladstone as liberal premier, social reform might have come in England nearly twenty years sooner than it did. In that case the labour party – at least in the form which it actually took – might never have been born".[206]

Subsequently, the efforts of Winston Churchill and of Lloyd George to blur the barriers between old style laissez-faire Liberalism and demands for social reform were unlikely to appeal to most of their colleagues within the Liberal Cabinet. "Men like McKenna, Runciman and Grey, seemed utterly out of sympathy with the collectivist creed. Asquith himself supplied no new initiatives; he was a man who responded passively to political pressures from without."[207] Lloyd George and Churchill were never members of an 'Asquith-led' Political Committee. Furthermore, they resigned together from the

---

205 D A Nicholls, *The Lost Prime Minister A Life of Sir Charles Dilke* (London, 1995), pp.295/6.

206 Sir Robert Ensor, *England 1870-1914* (Oxford, Paperback edition, 1985 reprinted 1988), p.389.

207 K O Morgan, *The Age Of Lloyd George* (London, 1971), p.42.

Reform Club in January 1913 although not it seems, as was rumoured at the time, on political grounds.[208]

As might be expected of a Committee, whose Chairman continued to be Asquith until his death in 1928, 'Old Liberalism' and defensive politics tended to dominate. The prominent author and Liberal journalist, J A Spender, a friend and close supporter of Asquith, was an influential member of the Political Committee.[209] Stephen Koss, in his biography of another prominent Liberal editor, A G Gardiner, talks of the prevailing feeling at the Reform Club as "pro Asquith and anti Lloyd George."[210] Although the latter succeeded Asquith as leader of the Liberal Party in 1926, it was to the Marquis of Crewe the Political Committee turned for a successor to Asquith as Chairman in 1928. An analysis of its membership that year shows a majority composed of 'elder statesmen' and traditional Liberals, a number of them former MPs. There were at least ten members noted for their strong support for Asquith, but only six recorded as supporters, or more accurately erstwhile supporters, of Lloyd George.[211] Lack of success at the general election of 1929, ostensibly fought under Lloyd George's leadership, was followed by further division of the Party into three factions for the general election of October 1931, as Liberals quarrelled over whether to support a Labour led National government under Ramsay MacDonald following the financial and political crisis of the previous August. All thirty-five seats won by Sir John Simon's anti-Labour Liberal Nationalists in 1931 were to be dependent on Conservative votes in 1935 following the 'concordat' between the two established in advance of that general election campaign, and 'Simonites' were to go on to become indistinguishable from Conservatives. After the general election of 1935 'orthodox' Liberals could only muster twenty-one MPs.

Against this background it is not surprising to find a process of change in eligibility for membership of the Reform Club which, while gradual, was at

---

208 George Woodbridge claims persuasively that the reason behind their resignations was friendship for Baron Maurice Arnold de Forest, Liberal MP for West Ham North, who had been blackballed by members of the Reform Club. See Woodbridge, Reform Club p.91. Lloyd George rejoined the Club in 1917. Winston Churchill never returned.

209 Spender, a close friend also of Sir Edward Grey, edited the Westminster Gazette from 1896 to 1922 and published his biography of Asquith in 1932. The Reform Club gave two dinners for Spender, in 1928 and 1937, and commissioned a portrait in his honour.

210 Stephen Koss, Fleet Street Radical: A G Gardiner and the Daily News (London, 1973), p.202. Gardiner, a firmly Radical editor, became implacably opposed to Lloyd George during the Great War. He was elected to the Political Committee but not until 1931.

211 Political sympathies have been deduced from Who's Who Of Members of Parliament, Who's Who, and from published works on the period including biographies. Those of ten members have not been identified. At least nineteen members of the Political Committee of 1928 were aged seventy or older.

times perceived by members or candidates for membership as in need of clarification. The General Committee's ambivalent response to that request of Thomas Kennedy, as early as June 1886, for a ruling on whether he would be "justified in voting against the Party headed by Mr Gladstone",[212] was matched by an apparent refusal to accept the proffered resignation of Thomas Lauder Brunton in July 1895. Lauder Brunton admitted an intention to vote for a Conservative candidate in the general election of that month "as there was no Liberal Unionist in the field", adding later that he would leave the question of acceptance or not of his resignation in the hands of the Committee. Clearly the Committee was unwilling to accept it. For he remained a member until 1912 when he resigned again on the grounds of disagreement with Liberal policy over "the unity of kingdom and empire". On this occasion he did leave the Club.[213]

Regrettably there seems to be no trace of a response to Sir Arthur Conan Doyle's letters seeking a "formal and definite ruling" on whether a member of the Reform Club was within his rights in standing as a Liberal Unionist candidate for Parliament. There seems no reason why he should not have received an affirmative reply. No doubt he did so, for he remained a member until also adding his name to the resignations of 1911/12. Conan Doyle was not just a committed Unionist, but supported tariff reform, a platform which may well have been the reason for his failure to obtain election to the Political Committee in May 1906.[214] After the spate of resignations in 1911/1912, Charles Stanford, who was to sit as Unionist MP for Brighton from 1914 to 1920, and later joined the Carlton Club, is reported to have asked for guidance on whether he was obliged to resign from the Club on changing his political views. The Secretary was instructed to reply that "no rule governs the action of members in this respect and that it is left to your discretion to take the course you consider desirable under the circumstances".[215]

At another earlier time of a number of firm resignations from the Club (over the issues of imperialism and the South African war), the Reverend James Marchant received assurances from the Club's Secretary that membership of any political party did not rule out membership of the Reform Club. In his case the Secretary took refuge in setting out plainly the only conditions for eligibility which had ever formally applied:

---

212 See text associated with note 165.

213 Lauder Brunton to Secretary of Reform Club, 15 July and 18 December 1895, Lauder Brunton to Newbigging, 26 October 1912, Reform Club mss., Box 9.

214 Sir Arthur Conan Doyle to Newbigging, 29 September 1900 and (later) undated letter, Reform Club mss., Box 9. See also GC Minutes, 21 December 1911 and Lord James of Hereford to Lloyd Morgan, 30 May 1906.

215 Reform Club, GC Minutes, 4 December 1913.

". . . conditions under which you can become a candidate for this Club are: you must be a Reformer, and you must be proposed and seconded by two members one of whom must have personal knowledge of you".[216]

It was not, however, until 1926 that the General Committee passed a resolution ordering substitution of the words 'Strictly Liberals' by that of 'Reformers' in the description of the Club's membership in Whitakers Almanac and Club publications.[217] Associated with this decision must have been the concern over falling membership expressed in the Club's Annual Report the following year, and the discussion within the General Committee in early 1926 on the eligibility of members of the Labour Party. The latter gave rise to the only example after 1886 of any involvement by the Political Committee in the 'political eligibility', or otherwise, of individuals for membership of the Club. The General Committee's Vice-Chairman, Francis Mellor, was deputed to seek the formal advice of the Political Committee on the "desirability or otherwise of electing to membership of the Club a candidate who is; 1. a Labour Member of Parliament. 2. a Labour candidate for Parliament. 3. a Member of the Labour Party". At its meeting to consider this first really political issue to come its way since 1911, the Political Committee firmly 'batted the ball straight back'. Members approved a formal response that "the persons mentioned in the three categories are not necessarily ineligible for election, having regard to Rule 1", adding that "the desirability of election of any candidate rests with the General Committee".[218] Rule 1 described the Club as being one for "Reformers".

In May 1930 the General Committee resolved unanimously that there was no reason for a member to resign from the Club having joined the Conservative Party. However, less than a year later Lord Dickinson, previously Sir Willoughby Hyett Dickinson, Liberal MP for St Pancras North, resigned from the Political Committee, having recently joined the Labour Party. Dickinson's letter of resignation makes it clear that he was 'pushed rather than jumped', but evidently he considered his change of allegiance was no bar to retaining his membership of the Club.[219] This suggests that, however 'open-minded' the General Committee might have become over the political affiliation of members of the Club, the Political Committee continued to be the prerogative of those who styled themselves Liberals – of whatever sort – at least until after the Second World War.

The most open acknowledgement of change in the political eligibility of candidates for membership of the Club was expressed at the Annual General

---

216 *Club Secretary to James Marchant, Reform Club letter book, 17 December 1901.*

217 *Reform Club, GC Minutes, 7 July 1926.*

218 *Francis Mellor to Collins, 7 and 27 January 1926, Collins to Mellor, 10 February 1926, Reform Club mss., Box 9. See also Reform Club PC Minute Book 3, pp.278-282.*

219 *Lord Dickinson to Collins, 21 January 1931, Reform Club mss., Box 9.*

Meeting of 1932. The Vice-Chairman, Sir Alfred Dennis, moving the adoption of the annual report and accounts, stated:

> "We cannot rely upon our connection with the old Liberal Party for the maintenance of our former position. . . this Club is very dependent in the past and in its origin, upon its connection with a Political Party. The fortunes of that Party of late years have not been very happy and the result has been reflected in the character of the membership of this Club."[220]

Yet it was not until after the Second World War that the General Committee placed a rather more definitive interpretation upon eligibility for membership of the Club than had previously been available. It instructed that the proposer and seconder of the candidature of Thomas Skeffington-Lodge, member of the Fabian Society, trade unionist and Labour MP for Bedford, should be informed that it did not seem likely that their candidate would be elected. The Committee then went on to advise withdrawal of his candidature. That decision may or may not have been influenced solely by political considerations, but in his case the Committee went on to resolve:

> "That this Committee does not consider that membership of any Political Party is a bar to membership of the Club. The Committee does consider that a candidate who is an active member of a Political Party, and particularly an MP – other than a member of the Liberal Party – should be subject to the most careful scrutiny".[221]

Such a resolution gives credence to the view of George Woodbridge that withdrawal of the names of four prominent candidates between 1921 and 1942 was for political reasons. He may be right but, as in most cases of blackballing, the precise reasons for the withdrawal of most candidates must remain largely a matter of conjecture.[222]

The gradual movement away from a direct linkage with political Liberals may have had a bearing on the increase in the number of members of the Club, and in due course Political Committee, from the Public Services, although the expansion of those Services within a continuingly widening democracy will probably have played the major part. In 1973 Sir Richard Clarke examined the connection between distinguished civil servants and membership of the Reform Club. He concluded that while the number of members of the Club from the Home Services overtook those from India and other Services overseas at the beginning of the 20th Century, the major increase took place after the First World War. He concluded also that by 1936 individuals from the Public Services as a whole had become an important part

---

220 Reform Club, AGM Minutes, 5 May 1932.

221 Reform Club, GC Minutes, 13 June 1946. The nomination, proposed by John Dugdale MP, seconded by Lord Faringdon, and supported by Woodrow Wyatt, Guy Burgess and five others, was withdrawn. See Candidates' Book, August 1941-June 1946, p.471.

222 Woodbridge, Reform Club, pp.86/87.

of the Club's membership. Two other items of information taken from his review provide a flavour of the quality of those members and are perhaps worth quoting. First, that in the 1930s twelve members of future Permanent Secretary rank and seven others who reached that of Deputy Secretary joined the Club. Second, that in 1973 "probably about 20 very senior civil servants are members of the Reform Club and perhaps as many retired very senior civil servants".[223]

A Continuing Relevance?

In spite of, or perhaps because of, the apparent loss of an active political role, attacks upon the continuing relevance of the Political Committee have been rare. It was not until forty-six years after Mr Tagart's motion at the annual general meeting of 1885, that the Committee was challenged publicly again to justify its existence to the membership. Two entries in the Club's Suggestions Book, dated 24 April and 21 May 1931, read as follows:

"Could some information be given of the activities of the Political Committee during the past year, together with some indication as to how a committee of such divergent political views can have any effective united action as "reformers"?
24 April 1931. . ."

"Whereas members at the recent meeting of the Political Committee were given no opportunity of submitting names owing to the fact that no public notice was given of the deaths during the past year nor of the returning ten members, would the Political Committee have any objection to the immediate formation of a group of members entitled "The Minority Political Committee" who holding progressive views wish the Club to regain its position in the Political life of the community, and regret that, in spite no doubt of the efforts of the Political Committee, it has become merely a social centre with a first class restaurant?
21 May 1931 . . ."

The Political Committee's response, approved at a meeting the following July, was a comparatively lengthy one. It contained a list of its meetings, and those of its sub-committee, held between June 1930 and March 1931. It listed the major functions which the Committee had played a part in organising between 1928 and 1931, and rounded off its opening remarks by referring to the elections of the Marquesses of Reading and of Crewe as respectively Vice-Chairman and Chairman. The following extracts provide a flavour of the remainder of the Committee's line by line riposte:

---

223 Sir Richard Clarke KCB OBE, *The Reform Club and the Civil Service*, unpublished but dated November 1973 and held by the Reform Club's Librarian, pp.1, 6, 12, and 19.

"While the Committee includes representatives of different types of "Reformers" no serious divergence of view has been evident . . . the Liberal traditions of the Reform Club have been consistently observed. . . . The election of the Political Committee has taken place in accordance with Rule XV. Ten members retire annually, but unlike the General Committee they are eligible for re-election. . . Vacancies occurring during the year are filled up by the Committee. All the ten members due to retire this year were duly nominated in writing for re-election fourteen days before the Annual [General] Meeting as required by the rule. No other nominations were delivered to the Secretary of the Club. . . It would appear that the appointment of "The Minority Political Committee", as suggested, would require amendment of Rule XV. . . The Political Committee . . . already contains some of "progressive views" who share the desire of the signatories that the position of the Club in the political community should be maintained and who would regret that it should become merely a social centre with a first class restaurant."[224]

All in all a measured response which seems to have silenced those particular critics! It is perhaps also worth noting that these entries in the Suggestions Book coincide with an exchange of correspondence which has survived in the Club's archive and which is related to the division of the Liberal Party into three factions before the general election of October 1931. The letters, one of which is signed by Lord Crewe as Chairman, are particularly concerned with Sir John Simon's group of Liberal Nationalists, but include reference to a proposal that the Political Committee should provide an opportunity for Liberals of all persuasions to meet and air their differences across the dinner table. The only indication from the minutes of any practical result is reference to the appointment of a dinner sub-committee. However any initiative that might have been put in hand was no doubt overtaken by the general election and by concentration on arrangements for the banquet to commemorate the centenary of the Great Reform Act.[225]

This was not the only reference within the Suggestions Book to the Political Committee. In April 1949 the following suggestion was referred formally to the Political Committee by the General Committee, presumably with collective tongue firmly in collective cheek:

"Since avowed supporters of the Conservative and Socialist Parties have been admitted to the Club it has become necessary to lock up the new library books and hard to obtain an adequate meal unless one

---

224 Reform Club, PC Minute Book 3, pp.334-338. See also the memorandum attached to Collins to C Hope-Johnstone, 14 May 1931, Reform Club mss., Box. 9.

225 Collins to Lord Crewe, confidential undated letter, Crewe to Collins, 20 May 1931, Collins to Sir Robert Hadfield, 23 May 1931, Hadfield to Collins, 27 May 1931, together with assorted newspaper cuttings, Reform Club mss., Box 9. See also PC Minute Book 3, p.332.

hastens with indecent greed to grab a place in the dining room at 1pm or 7pm precisely . . . Would it not be advisable to revive and strengthen the Political Committee and interpret the qualification of Reformer with more stricture?"

At its next meeting the Political Committee decided that this suggestion should "lie on the table."[226] However, enforced political inactivity clearly rankled with some of its members. At the same meeting a sub-committee was formed to review the Political Committee's own activities, the first in a series of fresh initiatives to examine the case for a more active political role. Most notably the Committee held an 'internal' dinner on 31 January 1952, at which its members discussed whether, in the light of "the inactivity of the Committee during recent years", the membership of the Club should be invited "to amend the constitution by winding up the Political Committee. . ." The general view was that it would be wrong so to do. Further, that means of revising the Committee's activities through return to a series of dinners and discussion meetings, with guests invited to participate, should be put in hand. This seems to have been the first time that the word 'Liberal', as opposed to 'Reformer', was openly divorced from a party political meaning. The record of the discussion at the dinner includes the following extract:

". . . It was stressed that the Reform Club is a Club of the Reformers of the United Kingdom and contains in its membership persons claiming to share a common Liberal outlook, although attached as individuals to various political parties or to none. . ."[227]

In 1953 a grant was requested to offset expenses. However, these were not detailed and there seems to be no record of the General Committee's response. At meetings in 1964 and 1968 the absence of any entitlement by members of the Political Committee to take part in political activities on behalf of the Club was recorded formally in the minutes. Nevertheless, on the subject of its relationship with politics, the Committee placed on record in 1970 its own view that the ". . .Liberal element in the Political Committee should not be allowed to lapse. . .its members could continue to hold and voice Liberal views without having any party affiliation."[228]

It is evident that the attempt in 1911 to revive any overtly political role on the part of the Club was overtaken by the First World War and the further divisions which rocked the Liberal Party both during and after that war. While the decline in the number of serving MPs on the Committee was never reversed, membership by Liberal Chief Whips and even Cabinet Ministers continued. In fact it could be said that nearly all prominent Liberal politicians

---

226 Reform Club, PC Minute Book 4 (the current minute book), 23 May 1949.

227 Extract from copy of a Report of a Dinner held by the Political Committee, Reform Club, PC Minute Book 4, 31 January 1952.

228 Reform Club, PC Minute Book 4, 21 May 1953, 13 April 1964, 30 April 1968, and 27 April 1970.

in the post-First World War era were members at one time or another, with the notable exception of David Lloyd George; a tribute to the continuingly powerful symbolic place of the Reform Club at the heart of political Liberalism, at least until the Second World War. The overall flavour of the Committee in that era was, however, that of a traditional Liberalism, possibly a natural consequence of the continuing chairmanship of Asquith until the year of his death. These years also saw the very gradual but formal acceptance of members of the Club from all political parties as the fortunes of the Liberal Party continued to wane. Such a move was no doubt inevitable if the membership was to remain at a viable level, particularly after the Second World War, and has led to the apolitical nature of to-day's Reform Club including that of its now apparently inaptly named Political Committee.

CONCLUSION

Writing in commemoration of its Silver Jubilee, a member described the Reform Club as "a focus of Liberal thought, a stronghold of unity and a healer of divisions".[229] Yet such a description was surely a contradiction in terms when applied to the diverse ranks of the Liberal Party. Either unity could be bought at the expense of focus, or focus would bring conflicts of policy and priorities thus destroying unity. Certainly Edward Dicey, editor of the Observer from 1870 to 1899, saw this flaw at the heart of political Liberalism. He declined nomination for membership of the Reform by its Political Committee in 1886, on the grounds that it would curtail full liberty of comment and criticism, and went on to comment some months later: "Do I care more about the Liberals being in power, or about the maintenance of the principle which forms the basis of all true Liberalism. As a Liberal, and because I am a Liberal, I am bound to choose the latter alternative".[230] The record shows that Dicey was not alone in that belief, although less prone perhaps than many to self delusion in respect of its political consequences. Parliamentary majorities of all Liberal Administrations between 1832 and the beginning of the 20th Century collapsed into squabbling factions which surrendered power to the Conservatives, seemingly often accompanied by a huge collective sigh of relief.

The parliamentary Radical initiators of a Club for Reformers had envisaged a party political headquarters from which a Whig dominated status quo could be forced to make way for progressive policies. In contrast the Club's political history developed into one of periodic calls for action lost among a membership which preferred the half-hearted approach of a Whiggish Russell, the cynically able leadership of a conservative Palmerston, the political balancing act of an ambiguous Gladstone, and the traditional Liberalism of a defensive Asquith. On one side were those who believed that an activist, progressive and co-ordinated role on the part of the Liberal Party was probably impossible, and certainly inappropriate. Opposed to them was an apparent minority increasingly convinced of the need to form a more representative party political organisation in an age of growing interdependence between expanding local associations and their Members of Parliament. In the absence of any other meaningful institution for the purpose, this latter group made several unsuccessful attempts to galvanise the Club into action before a Political Committee was formed in the wake of the Second (Conservative) Reform Act of 1867.

As a conduit for entry into Parliament, for patronage and for political status, membership of the Reform Club, perhaps particularly of its Political

---

229 Fagan, The Reform Club, p.137.

230 Edward Dicey, 'The Plea of a Malcontent Liberal,' Fortnightly Review, XXXVIII, New Series (October 1885), p.467.

Committee, had few rivals for many years. By definition such characteristics added an air of exclusiveness, even mystery, but at the price of conformity, and conformity tended to muffle the Reformist role explicit in the title and original political conception of the Club. It encouraged that "extraordinary monotony of opinion", which pervaded the 'solid centre' of wealthy Liberal backbenchers, whether directly connected or not with the landed interest.[231] Meanwhile this perceived exclusiveness on the part of such an unrepresentative institution as a metropolitan club bred resentment and suspicion within an increasingly educated, articulate and politically aware population served by an expanding regional Press, and whose access to the franchise had been substantially extended by the Reform Act of 1867. This militated against any active role within constituencies, the primary raison d'etre for the Committee's existence. The making of policy was not an option. In the Gladstonian era this was never allowed to escape from the firm control of the leadership.

Thus the plurality of Liberalism and the ethos of Club combined to frustrate any obviously meaningful contribution to the cause of Reform. Many members saw other than very cautious steps in that direction as a drive towards an irreversible democracy which could threaten land, property, the freedom of bequest, and perhaps even destroy the reasoned debate of an enlightened Parliament itself. By the late 1870s Radicals, themselves divided into factions by differences over legislative priorities, had sought a solution at the level of the constituency through the politics of the 'Caucus'. This was a system unacceptable to the Whig hierarchy of the Liberal Party, and even to its mainstream traditionalist followers, as a denial of true Liberalism. Hopes of a Liberal club at the heart of Radical politics were not abandoned. The founding of the National Liberal Club in 1882 reflected a confidence among Radicals that the politics of the future belonged to them, and that a new start was needed.

During its politically active phase between 1869 and 1886, initiatives of any consequence from within the Political Committee of the Reform Club failed to achieve the support of the majority. On occasions they led to actual disharmony among the membership. Attempts at arbitration between conflicting Liberal candidates, in accordance with the Committee's terms of reference, usually aroused unfavourable and undesirable publicity in the newspapers. Initiation of resolutions to expel members on political grounds, seemingly based as much on the 'unattractive' conduct or personality of the individual concerned, should probably have been left to the membership of the Club as a whole. There remains the extent to which the Political Committee may have exercised some meaningful political power through association, the deployment of the influence of the dinner table or 'smoke-filled room'. Clearly this is largely unquantifiable but the impartial observer

---

231 *Vincent, Formation of the British Liberal Party*, p.63.

should beware of entering that world of mystery bred of suspicion, conjecture and the resentment of the excluded. Such a world involves the extravagant language of speculative provincial or militantly Radical journalism, even the fiction of Trollope's <u>Phineas Finn</u> or Disraeli's <u>Coningsby.</u>

During the 19th Century, there was certainly a perception of the political 'power' of the Club. Charles Dickens wrote in 1841 of Liberal MPs "bound hand and foot to the Reform Club", but he was not a member. The journalist and editor, T Wemyss Reid, described the Reform in 1882 as "the 'Ministerialist' Club", but he was not to be prominent in its committees for several years afterwards.[232] Certainly the Club was the primary social centre for Liberals in general, and it became a focus for marking the achievements of international freedom movements, for example those of Italy and of the slaves of the Confederacy. Following the formation of a Political Committee, it also became the natural choice of location for Liberals to meet in order to elect their leaders and for those leaders to seek votes of confidence when under pressure from within the Party. Yet all this is largely symbolic. It can hardly be said of itself to have meant much in the context of policy making, or the actual business of government.

The bulk of those who served on the Political Committee during the 19th and early 20th Century, and more importantly of the less than one-third of its membership who regularly attended meetings, were from middle class commercial and professional backgrounds. Many might be described as "shades of Liberal with a strong municipal accent . . . election-platform, aldermanic-bench, back-bench classes".[233] Here may lie the key to the major contribution made by the Political Committee of the Reform Club, perhaps one not all that far removed from the hopes of its Radical founders or, for that matter, the plans of their Whig 'colleagues' of that time. For the Committee helped to 'bring forward' the politician of the middle class. It assisted in the process of broadening by consent, in contrast to revolutionary developments in much of the rest of Europe, the representative nature of a legislature whose membership up to the middle of the 19th Century had been largely dictated by a landowning aristocracy; a start, if a modest one, to the marriage of popular control in an increasingly politicised nation with the cultural dominance of property.

It is perhaps a pity that such protagonists of the partnership of capital and labour in the industrial field as J P Brown Westhead, M T Bass, A J Mundella, Samuel Morley, and J W Pease, influential within both Party and Political Committee, were unable either to see, or perhaps to persuade others to see, the political place of organised labour as something more than just

---

232 M House and G Storey (ed.), <u>Letters of Charles Dickens, </u>Pilgrim ed. (7 vols., London, 1969), Vol 2 (1840-1841), p.304, Reid (ed.), <u>Memoirs of Wemyss Reid 1842-1855,</u> p.324.

233 C Binfield, 'Nonconformity's True Conformity', in T C Smout (ed.), Victorian Values A Joint Symposium of the Royal Society and the British Academy December 1990, <u>Proceedings of The British Academy,</u> LXXVIII, (Oxford, 1990), p.95.

another sectional and minority lobby of the Party, like temperance or Nonconformity, or even the national interests of Welsh and Scottish Liberalism. In relating themselves to the landed aristocracy, middle class Liberals succeeded, if slowly, in laying the foundation for changes in the composition of the House of Commons. Similar development of a meaningful rather than token relationship with organised labour, in order to absorb their representatives into Parliament, the whole bolstered by the practical effects of an expanding educational service, wider religious tolerance and a growing provincial press, could have taken the process further. At the same time it might have started the process of integrating fully those forces into the Liberal Party, instead of setting the scene for their ultimate alienation and, in time, the very politics of class warfare they affected to oppose. But all this is to be wise after the event. Such a transformation would have needed a fundamental change in the attitude of many at the level of the constituency. Furthermore, and perhaps even more importantly, it ignores the predominant influence of Gladstone in the politics of the time. It discounts his cautious approach to any course which might undermine the principle of a political leadership based on the essential nature of social rank to the continuance of a civilised society.

Within the Reform Club itself the advent of a new ideological division in 1886 was quick to reinforce the view of the majority that for Liberals the collective pursuit of the politics of party should be largely excluded from its walls. Further, that the very survival of such a famous international symbol of political freedom and plurality depended on such lack of action. The number of serving MPs on the Political Committee declined sharply and it was not until 1911 that the Committee rediscovered a role through the organisation of dinners of a 'political character' intended to advance the Liberal cause. These continued in the years between the two great wars, and were usually confined to members of the Political Committee and their guests. For the General Committee increasingly represented a Club membership drawn from across the political spectrum and from the growing Public Services, as fresh divisions continued to weaken the Liberal Party. It is noteworthy that during this later period of largely symbolic Liberal representation, and perhaps a reflection of the chairmanship of Asquith, an 'upgrading' in political terms of membership of the Political Committee seems to have taken place. Most leading Liberal figures of the 1920s and indeed 1930s, with the noteworthy exception of David Lloyd George, seem to have been members.

Following the Second World War the trend towards an apolitical institution quickened. Prominence within the membership of the Political Committee finally passed completely from politicians (or by the late 1940s largely 'retired' politicians) to 'laymen', including members of academic institutions and of the rapidly growing public services needed to serve the voracious demands of a still expanding democracy. Paradoxically it may be that the influence of the membership of Club, if not necessarily of the

Political Committee, on public policy actually grew as a result. George Woodbridge quotes from the memoirs of Lord Chandos of a need by the mid twentieth century for ministers to be on such terms with their senior officials "as to know what is being agreed or disputed at lunch in the Reform Club or the Athenaeum by the Heads of the Civil Service".[234] His comment receives some backing from the figures quoted in Sir Richard Clarke's unpublished review of membership of the Club on the part of civil servants, which is held by the Club's Librarian. The Political Committee's move away from an open collective identification with the cause of political Liberalism took rather longer than that of the Club as a whole. Nevertheless, to-day's Committee, which meets periodically to dine and discuss current affairs, owns to no political identity and is no doubt content to stand on the views of its predecessor of 1970 that members are not required to have a 'party affiliation'.

---

234 Oliver Lyttleton, Viscount Chandos, *The Memoirs of Lord Chandos* (London, 1962), p.349 and quoted at Woodbridge, *Reform Club*, p.35.

APPENDIX 1   (refers to page 3)

ADMINISTRATIONS FROM REFORM ACT OF 1832 TO SECOND WORLD WAR.

Whig[1], Earl Grey, new and Reformed Parliament met for first time in 1833.

Whig, Viscount Melbourne, July 1834 on Grey's retirement.

Conservative[2], Sir Robert Peel, December 1834 on 'dismissal' of Melbourne by the King and subsequently an election, although Peel's supporters were in a minority.

Whig, Viscount Melbourne, April 1835 after several defeats of Peel in Parliament and confirmed at election of 1837.

Conservative, Sir Robert Peel, September 1841 on defeat of Melbourne in Parliament and confirmed at election.

Whig, Lord John Russell, July 1846 on defeat of Peel in Parliament following the Split in the Conservative Party over Repeal of Corn Laws, and confirmed at election.

Conservative, Earl of Derby, February 1852 on defeat of Russell in Parliament.

Coalition (Peelites and Whigs), Earl of Aberdeen, December 1852 on defeat of Derby in Parliament after election the previous July had confirmed Derby in power.

Coalition (As above), Viscount Palmerston, February 1855 on Melbourne's resignation and reinforced by election of 1857.

Conservative, Earl of Derby, February 1858 on defeat of Palmerston in Parliament.

Liberal[3], Viscount Palmerston, June 1859 following defeat of Derby in Parliament and elections both in 1859 and again in July 1865.

Liberal, Earl (formerly Lord John) Russell, October 1865 on Palmerston's death.

Conservative, Earl of Derby, June 1866 on Russell's resignation following defeat in Parliament.

Conservative, Mr Disraeli, February 1868 on Derby's retirement through illness.

1 Selection of the description of 19th Century Administrations is a subjective judgement based on the overall thrust of its leadership. For example, Lord Melbourne's Administration of April 1835 was of a fundamentally Whig character although 'backed' by Radicals and Irish repealers, while it is particularly difficult to fix too precise a 'label' on the Administrations of the 1850s, and most of those of the 1860s, when political loyalties were very loose.

2 Use of the word 'Conservative' as a political description was used for the first time by George Canning in 1824. However, the Administration of Sir Robert Peel is generally accepted as the first Conservative one, following his 'Tamworth Manifesto' of 1834, which promoted moderate reforms while continuing to support a due respect for established institutions.

3 While the term 'Liberal' began to be widely used in politics in the early 1830s, Lord Palmerson's introduction of Radicals, not just into his Cabinet but more generally into government office in his second Administration, together with his personal popularity in the country at large, could be said to entitle him to be described as the first Liberal Prime Minister. However, some would argue this to be a 'title' more properly belonging to the whiggish Russell, or more justifiably to Gladstone, although it should be pointed out that even the latter's Cabinets, up to 1886 at least, were dominated by Whigs!

Liberal, Mr Gladstone, December 1868 following general election.
Conservative, Mr Disraeli, February 1874 following general election.
Liberal, Mr Gladstone, April 1880 following general election.
Conservative, Marquess of Salisbury, June 1885 following defeat of Gladstone in Parliament.
Liberal, Mr Gladstone, February 1886 following general election and hung Parliament in December 1885.
Conservative, Marquess of Salisbury, August 1886 following defeat of Gladstone in Parliament over Home Rule for Ireland and general election fought on the Unionist issue.
Liberal, Mr Gladstone, August 1892 following general election.
Liberal, Earl of Rosebery, March 1894 on Mr Gladstone's retirement.
Conservative,[4] Marquis of Salisbury, June 1895 following general election.
Conservative, Marquis of Salisbury, following 'khaki' general election of October 1900.
Conservative, Mr Balfour, July 1902 on retirement of Marquis of Salisbury.
Liberal, Sir Henry Campbell-Bannerman, on resignation of Balfour in December 1905 and confirmed by general election.
Liberal, Mr Asquith, April 1908 on death of Campbell-Bannerman.
Liberal,[5] Mr Asquith, January 1910 following general election.
Liberal, Mr Asquith, December 1910 following general election.
Coalition, Mr Asquith, May 1915 on wartime 'front bench deal' with Conservatives.
War, Mr Lloyd George, December 1916, on Asquith's resignation as Prime Minister.
War,[6] Mr Lloyd George, January 1919, following 'coupon' general election.
Coalition, Mr Lloyd George, November 1919 on restoration of peacetime Cabinets.
Conservative, Mr Bonar Law, October 1922 following general election.
Conserative, Mr Baldwin, May 1923 on Bonar Law's resignation.
Labour, Mr Ramsay MacDonald, January 1924 following general election, but Labour only second largest party in House of Commons, the Conservatives being the largest.

---

4 *'Conservative' is used as short title for this effectively first 'Conservative and Unionist' Administration.*

5 *Liberal led Administrations between 1910 and 1915 relied on Labour and Irish Nationalists for an overall majority in the House of Commons.*

6 *Lloyd George's 'War' and Coalition Cabinets of 1919 were backed by an overall majority of Conservatives in Parliament. In fact the Conservatives secured majorities in five of the seven general elections held between the First and Second World Wars and in the others, those of 1923 and 1929, won the largest share of the vote. "The result of 1918 broke the [Liberal] Party, not only in the House of Commons but in the Country. Local associations perished or maintained a nominal existence. Masses of our best men passed away to Labour, others gravitated to Conservatism or Independence": (attributed to Herbert Gladstone by Chris Cook in his <u>Short History of the Liberal Party</u> (London, 1976), p.81, and also quoted at Pearce and Stewart, <u>British Political History 1867-1990</u>, p.223.*

Conservative, Mr Baldwin, November 1924 following the 'Zinoviev Red Letter' general election.
Labour, Mr Ramsay MacDonald, June 1929 following general election, and with Labour the largest party in Parliament although not with the largest share of the vote.
National, Mr Ramsay MacDonald, August 1931 as a result of the economic crisis.
National, Mr Ramsay MacDonald, November 1931 following general election, but which resulted in an overwhelming Conservative majority in Parliament.
National, Mr Baldwin, June 1935 on Ramsay MacDonald's resignation as Prime Minister.
National, Mr Baldwin, November 1935 following general election.
National, Mr Chamberlain, May 1937 on retirement of Baldwin.
War, Mr Chamberlain, September 1939.

APPENDIX 2   (refers to pages 25 and 78)

MEMBERS OF REFORM CLUB'S POLITICAL COMMITTEE ELECTED MAY 1869.[1]

Mainstream Liberal Mps

Brown Westhead J P (1807-1877). Merchant. 1st Chairman Political Committee. Pro Irish Church disestablishment, Ballot and partnership of capital and labour. (6S).[2]
Caird J (1816-1892). Agriculturist. Minister 1869-91.[3] Originally stood as Lib-Con. Chairman General Committee 1880-84. Pro public service retrenchment. (46R).
Coleridge Sir J (1821-1894). Barrister. Minister 1871-4. Lord Chief Justice 1880-94. Lost Nonconformist support by refusing to support abolition of church rates. (21S).
Collier Sir R P (1817-1886). Barrister. Knighted 1863. Minister 1859-70. Judge 1871. Pro Ballot. Actively assisted Chief Whip at 1868 general election. (42S).
Crawford R W (1813-1889). India merchant. Deputy governor Bank of England. Chaired Garibaldi's Reception Committee. Pro Irish Church disestablishment and Ballot. (5S).
Glyn G G (1824-1887). Banker. Chief Whip 1868-74. Paymaster General 1880-85. Single minded in Gladstone's support. Pro Ballot and abolition of church rates. (1R).
Goldsmid Sir F H (1808-1878). Barrister. First Jew called to English Bar. Founded Anglo-Jewish Association in 1871. Opposed to all religious endowments. (26S).
Hardcastle J A (1815-1894). Barrister. Close associate of Chief Whip and actively helped Glyn at the general election of 1868. Pro Irish Church disestablishment. (3R).
Henderson J (1807-1884). Carpet manufacturer and colliery owner. Prominent in supporting non-intervention in foreign policy. Pro abolition of

---

1 Ninety-six members entered the ballot for the fifty places. Descriptions of individuals, taken from biographical information or contemporary comments, have been restricted to a maximum of three lines per person and are primarily concerned with their situation in 1869. The preponderance of lawyers is hardly surprising. One-sixth of the House of Commons or over one hundred MPs were lawyers in the 1860s. Even in 1874 over half of these were Liberals.

2 The figures in brackets at the end of each individual's particulars show the place he achieved in the ballot for election to the Political Committee. For example, George Glyn received the most votes of club members, T R Williams the least among those successful in the ballot. The letter 'R' or 'S' immediately following those figures signifies the individual's record of attendance at meetings while a member of the Committee. 'R' signifies regular attendance and 'S' that the individual seldom or ever attended a meeting. Aside from association with the whips' office, there seems to be no obvious political significance to the number of votes either the individual himself or his grouping received, nor to comparative attendance levels between groupings.

3. Dates against ministerial appointments show the earliest and latest years such appointments were held. They are not intended to suggest the individual concerned remained a minister over the whole period.

church rates. (11R).

Hodgkinson G (1818-1881). Solicitor. Moved amendment extending vote to all borough householders in 1867 Act. Pro Irish Church disestablishment and short parliaments. (8R).

Leatham E A (1828-1900). Banker. Independent Liberal. Prominent in Club affairs. Chairman General Committee 1885-88. Liberal Unionist after 1886. (7R).

Locke J (1805-1880). Barrister. Southwark trader's son elected for borough (1857) but rejected by Liberal 200 in 1880. Pro short parliaments and household suffrage. (33R).

Onslow G J H (1814-1882). Soldier from a military family. Pro short parliaments, Ballot and abolition of church rates. (45S).

Otway Sir A J (1822-1912). Barrister. 3rd Bart. Minister 1868-71. Resigned over foreign policy. Deputy Speaker 1883. Pro assimilation of county and borough franchise. (28S).

Pease Sir J W (1828-1903). Merchant. First Quaker to accept honour from Crown. Pro partnership capital and labour yet political economist. Pro Irish Home Rule. (49R).

Young A W (1814-1885). Solicitor. Practised law in Australia becoming High Sheriff of New South Wales from 1842 to 1849. Pro Irish Church disestablishment. (13R).

Irish Liberal MPs[4]

Cogan W H F (1823-1894). Barrister. Prominent Irish Catholic but one of only twelve Irish MPs against Home Rule at 1874 election. Vice-Chairman Political Committee. (19R).

Esmonde Sir J (1826-1876). Barrister and major of militia. Whip 1866. Never actually joined Home Rule League and no record of ever supporting it in Parliament. (32S).

Murphy N D (1811-c1880). Solicitor. Supported Home Rule at Cork by-election December 1872 in order to gain re-election but finally disassociated himself in 1876. (43R).

O'Brien Sir P (1823-1895). Barrister. Originally supported Repeal of Union, but only joined Home Rule League prior to election of 1874 in order to gain re-election. (27S).

Sullivan Sir E (1822-1884). Barrister. Irish Solicitor General and Lord Chancellor. Firm adherent of Liberal Party. Detested by extreme advocates of Home Rule. (29S).

---

4 For much of the detail on the Irish Liberals see D A Thornley, *Isaac Butt and the Home Rule Party* (London, 1964), pp.196/7.

MPs of 'Whig Principles'

Brand Sir H (1814-1892). 23rd Baron Dacre (1890). Chief Whip 1859-66. In 1861 formed Liberal Registration Association. Chairman Political Committee 1871-2. Speaker 1872-83. (2 R) .
Cowper-Temple W F (1811-1888). 2nd son 5th Earl Cowper. Minister 1846-66. Baron Mount Temple (1869). Moved compromise motion on 1870 Education Act. (9S).
Dalhousie Earl (1801-1874). 11th Earl (1860). Minister 1846. Firm supporter of Gladstone as only man who could unify the Liberal Party. (40S).
Ebury Lord (1801-1893). 3rd son Marquis of Westminster. Founded Prayer Book Revision Society. Introduced Bill for Amendment of Act of Uniformity. (10S).

'Palmerstonian' Radical MPs[5]

Bass M T (1799-1884). Brewer. Advocated partnership capital and labour. Active promoter of railway trade unionism. Financial supporter Reform League. (19S).
Baxter W E (1825-1890). Scottish merchant. Minister 1863-73. Resigned from Treasury (1873). Landowner but anti-Whig. 'Took up' T Wemyss Reid of Leeds Mercury. (35R).
Bulwer Sir H L (1804-1872). Diplomat. Ambassador to Turkey (1858). Returned to England in 1865. Baron Dalling and Bulwer 1871. Lord Palmerston's biographer. (30S).
Crossley Sir F (1817-1872). Manufacturer. Baronetcy (1863). Dissenter. Pro Ballot and Irish Church disestablishment. Dismissed as 'rich political booby' by Cobden. (17S).
Dalgluish R (1808-1880). Scottish calico printer. Dissenter. Against grants for religious purposes. Pro Irish Church disestablishment. (31S).
Gibson T M (1807-1884). Minister 1846-8. Cabinet 1859-66 having opposed Palmerston in past. One time Tory MP (1837-39). Corn law repealer. Firm Gladstone supporter. (36S).
Gilpin C (1815-1874). Publisher. Minister 1859-65. Dissenter. Formed pact with Whig at Northampton (1868) to keep Bradlaugh out. Pro public expenditure economy. (18S).

---

5 *The categorisation of these Radical MPs under the head of 'Palmerstonian' dates from 1859. It reflects their transition to a ministerialist political position during his Second Administration, much to the irritation of Richard Cobden and John Bright who, by 1863, had been left largely isolated on the Radical wing of the parliamentary Liberal party. They include such men as Bass, Baxter and Jackson who were among those disgruntled middle class representatives of industrial boroughs who were successful in persuading Palmerston to broaden the basis of a Liberal government and thus re-unify the parliamentary party. They even include Milner Gibson who had actually been the main architect of Palmerston's downfall in February 1858. Ministerial office in the case of Gilpin and Stansfeld, a baronetcy for Crossley, and Cabinet office for Gibson and Villiers were to be 'followed up' later by Gladstone with office for Baxter and a baronetcy for Jackson.*

Jackson Sir W (1805-1876). Africa Merchant and railway contractor. Baronetcy (1869). Pro Ballot. (12R).
Seely C (1803-1887). Flour Mill owner. Influential Lincoln Radical but another who moderated his Radicalism in the 1860s. (22R).
Stansfeld Sir J (1820-1898). Barrister. Minister 1863-71. Cabinet 1871-4. Pro Italian republic. Dissenter. Supporter Reform League. Anti Contagious Diseases Act. (16S).
Villiers C P (1802-1898). Barrister. Minister 1852-58. Cabinet 1859-66. Prominent free trader. Chairman of Political Committee for twenty-six years. (25R).

'Independent' Radical MPs

Bright Jacob (1821-1899). Cotton manufacturer. Brother of John Bright. Dissenter. Firm advocate of women's rights. Consistent supporter Gladstone's Irish policy. (14S).
Hibbert J T (1824-1908). Barrister. Minister 1872-92. President County Councils Association. Knighted 1893. Pro Irish and Scottish Churches' disestablishment. (36R).
Morley S (1809-1886). Manufacturer. Proprietor Daily News. Dissenter but resigned Liberation Society. Pro partnership capital and labour. Supporter Reform League. (37R).
Potter T B (1817-1898). Merchant. Dissenter. Free trader. Established Cobden Club (1866) but supported Crimean War. Supporter Reform League. Friend of Garibaldi. (23R).

Non-MPs[6]

Baxter R (1811-1880). Barrister. 'The ideal committee man'. Served also on Club's General Committee for twenty-two years, seven as Chairman 1873-80. (4R).
Beare W G (1805-1873). Soldier. Served also on Club's General Committee, six years as Chairman 1867-73. (39S).
Cooper W D (1812-1875). Solicitor, author and antiquary. Journalist for Morning Chronicle and The Times. Solicitor to the Reform Club on its founding. (47S).
de la Pryme C (1815-1899). Barrister and author. Member of Reform Club's Political Committee for over thirty years. (15R).
Evans W. Mancunian merchant. Dissenter. (41R).
Morris Sir L (1833-1907). Barrister, poet, scholar. A pioneer of Education Movement in Wales. Vice-Chairman of Political Committee. (48R).
Norton T. Barrister. At one time Chief Justice of Newfoundland. Chairman of Reform Club's General Committee 1860-1867. (44S).

6 It has not been possible to establish the backgrounds of all non-MPs. A number, for example W G Beare, stood for Parliament but were unsuccessful.

Probyn J W. (24S).
Rae W Fraser (1835-1905). Barrister and author. One time overseas correspondent for Daily News. Chairman Club's Library Committee for thirty-two years 1873-1905.(34R).
Williams T R. Barrister. Member of Club's General Committee 1869. (50S).

APPENDIX 3 (refers to page 62)

EXTRACT FROM THE POLITICAL COMMITTEE'S REPORT OF 13 APRIL 1886[1].

"The Political Committee, as now constituted, was founded at the annual meeting of the Club in May 1869... The duties of the Political Committee were not defined in the resolution which constituted that body and which is to the effect that 'the Political affairs of the Club shall be managed by a Committee of fifty members.' At an early meeting the Committee drew up a series of resolutions defining their functions; these are '1' To promote the political organisation of the Liberal party and to add the several constituencies in securing suitable candidates for seats. '2' To arbitrate between conflicting Liberal Candidates at Parliamentary elections contesting the same seat or seats in order to prevent the loss of seats by division in the Liberal ranks.

'3' To suggest and carry out such changes in the rules and regulations of the Club as may from time to time be found necessary to secure its useful political action.

It was also resolved that the ordinary meetings of the Committee should take place on the first Tuesday in each month during the session of Parliament and that any two members should have the power to direct a meeting to be summoned for a special purpose.

When the Committee was originally constituted it was decreed that the number of its members should be fifty and that the quorum should be fifteen. It being found difficult to get fifteen members together, the rule was altered in 1871 when the quorum was fixed at seven. Since then the average attendance has been far in excess of that quorum and frequently attained the old quorum of fifteen.

At the General Meeting [of the Club] in 1877 another change was made in the rules affecting the Political Committee. The effect of this rule was to empower the Committee to elect two candidates in each year who had 'proved their attachment to the Liberal cause by marked and obvious services to it'. In accordance with that power, which is given in rule iv, the following candidates have been elected members of the Club:

1877   Professor Goldwin Smith: Mr J H Stoddart, editor of <u>The Glasgow Herald.</u>

1878   Mr Henry Dunckley, editor of <u>The Manchester Examiner & Times:</u>
Mr James Grahame then Hon Secty to the West of Scotland Liberal Association.

---

1 *The Report is reproduced verbatim, less the majority of its preamble which merely lists a number of past and present members of the Political Committee. See Reform Club, PC Minute Book 3, pp.36-46.*

1879   Mr A Craig Sellar, then Hon Secty to the Liberal Central Association:
The Earl of Breadalbane.
1880   Mr Thomas Burt MP:
Sir Peter Coats.
1881   Mr Edward Lloyd, Proprietor and Conductor of <u>Lloyds Weekly News</u> and the <u>Daily Chronicle:</u>
Mr Charles Cooper, editor of the <u>Scotsman.</u>
1882   Mr Henry Broadhurst MP.
1884   The Rt Hon G O Trevelyan MP.
1885   Mr Edward Dicey, editor of <u>The Observer:</u>
Mr H W Lucy now editor of <u>The Daily News.</u>
1886   The Rt Hon G J Shaw Lefevre:
Mr Herbert Gladstone MP.

A proof of the care of the Committee in selecting candidates is the fact that, although between 1877 & 1886, the Committee had the power to add twenty members to the Club, they elected sixteen only. As Mr Dicey declined to accept his election, the number of members added to the Club was fifteen, being five less than the number allowed by the rules. It is right to add that Mr Dicey's reason for not accepting his election was that, having been informed several members of the Club expressed strong disapproval of the election, he preferred rather than disturb the harmony of the Club - to decline the honour which had been conferred upon him and which he highly appreciated.

One candidate only [John Carvell Williams] has been rejected by a vote of the Committee. The rejection of this candidate was urged at the last annual meeting as a reason for summarily abolishing the Political Committee. However, as the reflection was chiefly due to the stringent proviso which obliges the Committee to be unanimous and gives any member the power to reject any candidate, it appears fair to conclude that the rejection of the candidate in question is a better reason for modifying the rule than for extinguishing the body which is governed by it.

The only specific complaint urged against the Political Committee at the annual meeting was to the effect that the Committee have expelled members from the Club. In a circular issued after the annual General Meeting and signed by Mr Villiers, the Chairman of this Committee, this charge was dealt with and answered in the following terms:- 'It is commonly but erroneously supposed that the Political Committee possess and have exercised exceptional powers as regards the expulsion of members. The truth is that any fifty members of the Club have precisely the same authority as that Committee; in other words, any fifty members may bring the conduct of any member before the General Committee. In all cases expulsion is the sole act of the General Committee, after a careful investigation of the facts, with the exception of those in which an appeal may be made to the Club in General Meeting, when the expulsion is due to a vote of the meeting.'

The Political Committee have steadily carried out the programme which they laid down after they were constituted and which is set forth early in this Report. Their task of promoting conciliation and harmony amongst the various sections and the several members of the Liberal party has been seriously pursued and, in many cases has been crowned with success; but the details, being confidential, cannot be disclosed. Amongst the useful work to which a clearer reference may be made without the betrayal of confidence, the most important is the service rendered to the Labour Representation League. A sub committee which conferred and arranged with a deputation from that League during 1870 comprised Mr Brand now Viscount Hampden and Mr Glyn now Baron Wolverton, while two members of the deputation, Mr Cremer and Mr Howell, are now members of Parliament. Another representative of the working classes, Mr Thomas Burt, MP, has been a member of this Club and of the Political Committee for several years.

In order to aid in consolidating the party, a deputation from this Committee united last October under the presidency of Lord Richard Grosvenor, now Baron Stalbridge [then Liberal Chief Whip], with deputations from the City Liberal Club, the National Liberal and the Devonshire Clubs to take steps for arbitrating between more than one Liberal candidate contesting the same seat. This joint body, representing the four Liberal Political Clubs of the Metropolis, resolved to establish a Board of Arbitration, which was accordingly done and which consisted of the Marquis of Hartington, Mr Chamberlain, Sir Henry James, Mr Samuel Morley and Mr John Morley, with power to add to their number.

Since the establishment of the Committee in 1869, the Chairmen have been Mr Brown-Westhead, Mr Brand, Mr C P Villiers, while the Vice-Chairmen have been the Rt Hon H F Cogan [W H F], Sir James Caird, Mr Grosvenor Hodgkinson, Mr J A Hardcastle, Mr Adolphus W Young, the Rt Hon W P Adam, Mr Lewis Morris and Lord Kensington. Till 1870 Mr Charles de la Pryme acted as honorary Secretary; since then the honorary Secretary has been Mr Fraser Rae.

As regards any change in the Committee's constitution, the Committee need only repeat what was stated in the circular issued to all the members of the Club last year, that 'the Committee would still heartily welcome - as they showed by their action they were ready to do in 1882 - any reform in their constitution which might benefit the Club, and prove of service to the Liberal party.'"

APPENDIX 4 (refers to page 63)

MEMBERS OF THE POLITICAL COMMITTEE IN JUNE 1886

Supporters of Home Rule/
Loyal to Gladstone
J B Balfour MP
J Barran MP (did not vote 8 June 1886)
Sir T Brassey MP
Jacob Bright (unseated 1885,
  re-elected 1886)
T Burt MP
Sir G Campbell MP
H Campbell-Bannerman MP
F A Channing MP
A Cohen MP
Sir C Dilke MP
J Dodds MP
Dr R Farquharson MP
J A Hardcastle (unseated 1885)
J T Hibbert MP (unseated 1886)
S Morley (retired as MP 1885, died Sep 1886)
Sir Lewis Morris
Sir A J Otway (retired as MP 1885)
J C Parkinson
Sir J W Pease MP
W Fraser Rae
Sir Charles Russell MP
C R Spencer MP
J Stansfeld MP
W Summers (unseated 1885, re-elected 1886)
J F Torr
W Woodall MP

Members Opposed to
Home Rule
J W Barclay MP
John Bright MP
L H Courtney MP
J Grahame
Lord Stalbridge (resigned Feb 1886)
Morgan Lloyd (unseated 1885)
F Pennington (retired as MP 1885)
P Rylands MP
R Horton Smith
C P Villiers MP
  (did not vote 8 June 1886)
A J Wright

Probable Supporters Of Home Rule
R J Biron
Sir J Caird (retired as MP 1885)
J Draper
Sir H Edwards (retired as MP 1885)
J F German
J Holms (retired as MP 1885)
Lord Kensington (unseated 1885)
Sir A Lusk (retired as MP 1885)
C T Macaulay

Probable Opponents Of Home Rule
C de la Pryme
F D Finlay
J Napier Higgins
C Seely (retired as MP 1885)

ABBREVIATIONS

AGM	Annual General Meeting
AP	Earl of Oxford and Asquith Papers
BBC	British Broadcasting Corporation
BL	British Library, Great Russell Street, London
BL C	British Newspaper Library, Colindale, London
CL B	Central Library, Bristol
CL M	Central Library, Manchester
CP	Richard Cobden Papers
DP	First Earl of Durham Papers
DU	Duke University, Durham, North Carolina
EC	Electoral Council of the Reform Club
GC	General Committee
GP	William Ewart Gladstone Papers
LCA	Liberal Central Association
LEA	Lambton Estate Archives
LRL	Labour Representation League
MoP	Sir William Molesworth Papers
MP	Member of the House of Commons
NLF	National Liberal Federation
NLS	National Library of Scotland, Edinburgh
PC	Political Committee
PP	Sir Robert Peel Papers
RP	Earl Russell Papers
SGM	Special General Meeting
UB	University of Bristol
UL	University of Leeds
UY	University of York
WCL	Wexford County Library

BIBLIOGRAPHY

1. Manuscript Sources

Earl of Oxford and Asquith Papers, BL, Add mss. 41210, Bodleian ms. 9
Richard Cobden Papers, BL, Add mss. 43649
First Earl of Durham Papers, DP, LEA, unreferenced correspondence
Edward John Stanley Papers, DU, unreferenced correspondence
Edward Ellice Papers, NLS, mss. 15044
Gladstone Library, UB, Minutes of LCA
William Ewart Gladstone Papers, BL, Add mss. 44193, 44194 & 44347
Sir William Molesworth Papers, Pencarrow, Unreferenced correspondence
National Liberal Club, Whitehall Place, Minutes of GC, AGM & SGM
Sir Robert Peel Papers, BL, Add mss. 40616
Reform Club, Pall Mall, Annual Reports, Members' Lists, Minutes of GC, PC, AGM, SGM, EC and unsorted correspondence
Earl Russell Papers, PRO, 30/22/25

2. Newspapers and Periodicals

Aberdeen Journal 1872, BL C
Beehive 1873, BL C
Bradford Daily Telegraph 1876, BL C
Chatham News 1865, BL C
Daily Telegraph 1886-7, BL C
Eastern Express 1870, BL C
Kelso Mail 1880, BL C
Leeds Mercury 1868-87, UL
Liberal And Radical 1887-9, UB
Liberal Magazine 1893-1916, UB
Manchester Guardian 1864-5, CL M
Reynolds Newspaper 1868-9, BL C
Speaker 1890-2, CL M
Spectator 1870-1892, CL B
The Times 1836-1912, UY
Western Gazette 1873, BL C
Wexford People 1874, WCL

Blackwoods Edinburgh Magazine 1872-82, UY
Bulletin of Institute of Historical Research 1954, UY
English Historical Review 1886-7, UY
Fortnightly Review 1868-85, UY
Historical Journal 1976, UY
Journal of Modern History 1945 and 1962, UY
Liberal Year Book 1887-9, UB

Liberal and Radical Year Book 1887-9, UB
Monthly Review 1904, CL M
Nineteenth Century 1878-1887, UY
Parliamentary History 1992, UY
Proceedings of British Academy 1990, UY
Quarterly Review 1856 and 1872-86, UY

3. Published Works

A Adburgham, A Radical Aristocrat: the Right Hon Sir William Molesworth Bart. PC. MP of Pencarrow and his Wife Andalusia (Padstow Cornwall, 1990).
Lord Askwith, Lord James of Hereford (London, 1930).
P H Bagenal, The Life of Ralph Bernal Osborne MP (London, 1884).
Michael Barker, Gladstone and Radicalism The Reconstruction of Liberal Policy in Britain 1885-94 Harvester Press ed. (Sussex, 1975).
Michael Bentley, The Climax of Liberal Politics British Liberalism in Theory and Practice 1868-1918 (London, 1987).
Michael Bentley, Politics Without Democracy 1815-1914, Fontana ed. Second Impression (London 1989).
W Besant, Fifty Years Ago (London, 1888).
Eugenio F Biagini and A J Reid (ed.), Currents of Radicalism Popular Radicalism, Organised Labour and Party Politics in Britain. 1850-1914 (Cambridge, 1991).
Eugenio F Biagini, Liberty, Retrenchment And Reform Popular Liberalism in the Age of Gladstone 1860-1880 (Cambridge, 1992).
Richard Brent, Liberal Anglican Politics: Whiggery, Religion and Reform 1830-1841 (Oxford, 1987).
Jessie K Buckley, Joseph Parkes Of Birmingham And The Part He Played In Radical Reform Movements From 1825 to 1845 (London, 1926).
Helen Colman, Jeremiah James Colman A Memoir (London, 1905).
G D H Cole, British Working Class Politics 1832-1914 (London, 1941).
C Cook, A Short History of the Liberal Party (London, 1976).
R A Cosgrove, The Rule of Law: Albert Venn Dicey, Victorian Jurist (London, 1980).
G W Cox, The Efficient Secret The Cabinet and the Development of Political Parties in Victorian England (Cambridge, 1987).
Major Curteis An Elector, Exposure Of The Corrupt System of Elections at Rye (London, 1853).
Michael Davitt, The Fall Of Feudalism In Ireland Or The Story Of The Land League Revolution (London, 1904).
T H Duncombe (ed.), The Life & Correspondence of Thomas Slingsby Duncombe Late MP for Finsbury (2 vols., London, 1868).
H S Eeles and Earl Spencer, Brooks's 1764-1964 (London, 1964).
Hon. Arthur D Elliot, The Life of George Joachim Goschen First Viscount

Goschen 1831-1907 (2 vols., London, 1911).
Sir Robert Ensor, England 1870-1914 (Oxford, 1936, paperback edition reprinted 1988).
T H S Escott, Edward Bulwer First Baron Lytton Of Knebworth: a Social, Personal and Political Monograph (London, 1910).
Louis Fagan, The Reform Club: its Founders and Architect (London, 1887).
Right Hon. R Farquharson, In and Out of Parliament - Reminiscences of a Varied Life (London, 1911).
Mrs Fawcett, Life of The Right Hon. Sir William Molesworth Bart. MP FRS (London, 1901).
Lord Edmond Fitzmaurice, The Life of Granville George Leveson Gower Second Earl Granville KG 1815-1891 (2 vols., London, 1905), Vol.2.
Sir Almeric Fitzroy, History of the Travellers Club (London, 1927).
M Freeden, The New Liberalism An Ideology Of Social Reform (Oxford, 1978).
Norman Gash, Politics In The Age Of Peel: a Study in the Technique of Parliamentary Representation 1830-1850 (London, 1961).
Norman Gash, Reaction and Reconstruction in English Politics 1832-1852 The Ford Lectures Delivered In The University Of Oxford In The Hilary Term 1964 (Oxford, 1965).
Stephen Gwynn MP and Gertrude M Tuckwell, The Life Of The Rt. Hon. Sir Charles Dilke (2 vols., London, 1917).
D A Hamer, Liberal Politics In The Age Of Gladstone and Rosebery: a Study In Leadership And Policy (Oxford, 1972).
D A Hamer, The Politics of Electoral Pressure A Study In The History of Victorian Reform Agitations Harvester Press ed. (Sussex, 1977).
Right Hon. Lord George Hamilton, Parliamentary Reminiscences & Reflections 1886-1906 (2 vols., London, 1922).
H J Hanham, Elections and Party Management Politics In The Time Of Disraeli And Gladstone Harvester Press ed. (Sussex, 1978).
Frederic Harrison, Autobiographic Memoirs (2 vols., London, 1911).
Christopher Harvie, The Lights of Liberalism: University Liberals and the Challenge of Democracy 1860-86 (London, 1976).
Thomas William Heyck, The Dimensions Of British Radicalism The Case of Ireland 1874-95 (Illinois, 1974).
Edwin Hodder, The Life of Samuel Morley (New York, 1888).
M House and G Storey (ed.), Letters Of Charles Dickens, Pilgrim ed. (7 vols., London, 1969), Vol 2 (1840-41).
T A Jenkins, Gladstone, Whiggery And The Liberal Party 1874-1886 (Oxford, 1988).
T A Jenkins, The Liberal Ascendancy (Basingstoke, 1994).
Trevor Lloyd, The General Election of 1880 (Oxford, 1968).
W C Lubenow, Parliamentary Politics And The Home Rule Crisis (Oxford, 1988).

H W Lucy, A Diary Of The Salisbury Parliament 1886-1892 (London, 1892).
J McCarthy (ed.), The Inner Life of the House of Commons, Richmond ed. (London, 1973).
Peter T Marsh, Joseph Chamberlain Entrepreneur In Politics (Yale, 1994).
H C G Matthew, Gladstone 1809-1874 (Oxford, 1986).
H C G Matthew (ed.), The Gladstone Diaries With Cabinet Minutes And Prime-Ministerial Correspondence Volume X January 1881-June 1883 (Oxford, 1990).
K O Morgan, The Age of Lloyd George (London, 1971).
John Morley, The Life of William Ewart Gladstone (3 vols., London, 1903).
Ian Newbould, Whiggery and Reform. 1830-41 The Politics of Government (Basingstoke, 1990).
David Nicholls, The Lost Prime Minister A Life of Sir Charles Dilke (Hambledon Press, 1995).
M Ostrogorski, Democracy and the Organisation of Political Parties (2 vols., London, 1902).
Jonathan Parry, The Rise and Fall of Liberal Government in Victorian Britain (Yale, 1993).
Malcolm Pearce and Geoffrey Stewart, British Political History 1867-1990 Democracy and Decline (London, 1992).
A E Pease, Elections and Recollections (London, 1932).
Henry Pelling, Social Geography of British Elections 1885-1910 (New York, 1967).
James Pope-Hennessey, Lord Crewe 1858:1945: The Likeness Of A Liberal (London, 1955).
Stuart J Reid, Life and Letters of The First Earl of Durham 1792-1840 (2 vols., London, 1906).
Stuart J Reid (ed), Memoirs of Sir Wemyss Reid 1842-1885 (London, 1905).
D Southgate, The Passing Of The Whigs 1832-1866 (London, 1962).
P Stanskey, Ambitions and Strategies In the Struggle for Leadership of the Liberal Party in the 1890s (Oxford, 1964).
E D Steele, Palmerston and Liberalism 1855-1865 (Cambridge, 1991).
Robert Steven, The National Liberal Club - Politics And Persons (London, 1920).
William Thomas, The Philosophic Radicals Nine Studies in Theory and Practice 1817-1841 (Oxford, 1971).
D A Thornley, Isaac Butt and The Home Rule Party (London, 1964).
Alger Labouchere Thorold, The Life of Henry Labouchere (London, 1913).
G M Trevelyan, Sir George Otto Trevelyan A Memoir (London, 1932).
John Vincent, The Formation of the British Liberal Party 1857-1868, Penguin ed. (Harmondsworth, 1972).
Sir Alexander West, Recollections 1832-1886, second ed. (2 vols., London, 1899).

George Woodbridge, The Reform Club 1836-1978 A history from the Club's records (Clearwater and Toronto, 1978).

4. Works Of Reference

Biographical Dictionary Of Modern British Radicals.
Boase's Modern English Biography.
Burke's Peerage.
Dictionary Of National Biography.
Dod's Parliamentary Companion.
McCalmont's Poll Book Of Parliamentary Constituencies.
Who Was Who.
Who's Who.
Who's Who Of British Members Of Parliament.